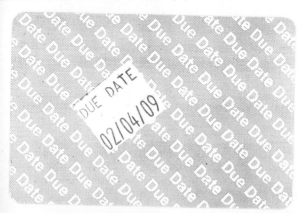

9/7/94
gift

IMPROVING PERFORMANCE

How to Manage
the White Space
on the Organization Chart

GEARY A. RUMMLER
ALAN P. BRACHE

IMPROVING PERFORMANCE

How to Manage
the White Space
on the Organization Chart

 Jossey-Bass Publishers

San Francisco • Oxford • 1991

IMPROVING PERFORMANCE
How to Manage the White Space on the Organization Chart
by Geary A. Rummler and Alan P. Brache

Copyright © 1990 by: Jossey-Bass Inc., Publishers
350 Sansome Street
San Francisco, California 94104
&
Jossey-Bass Limited
Headington Hill Hall
Oxford OX3 0BW

Library of Congress Cataloging-in-Publication Data

Rummler, Geary A.
    Improving performance : how to manage the white space on the
organization chart / Geary A. Rummler, Alan P. Brache.
        p.   cm — (The Jossey-Bass management serires)
    Includes bibliographical references.
    ISBN 1-55542-214-4
    1. Industrial productivity. 2. Performance. 3. Organizational
effectiveness. I. Brache, Alan P., date. II. Title.
III. Series.
HD56.R86   1990
658.4'02—dc20   89-43299
                                                                              CIP

Manufactured in the United States of America

The paper in this book meets the guidelines for
permanence and durability of the Committee on
Production Guidelines for Book Longevity of the
Council on Library Resources.

JACKET DESIGN BY WILLI BAUM

FIRST EDITION
    First printing: June 1990
    Second printing: January 1991
    Third printing: February 1991

Code 9042

THE JOSSEY-BASS
MANAGEMENT SERIES

Consulting Editors
Human Resources

Leonard Nadler
Zeace Nadler
College Park, Maryland

CONTENTS

PREFACE

American companies are playing in a ball game that is very different from the one they were winning fifteen, ten, and even five years ago. Most organizations are facing fierce global competition, which makes the competitive environment of the 1970s look like a gentlemanly game of cricket. To add to the pressure, many companies are faced with:

- Rapidly changing consumer demands for products and services. (Fifty percent of the services offered by major banks today did not exist ten years ago.)
- Increasing consumer demand for product quality and customer service. (For example, airline passengers require not only on-time arrival and speedy, gentle baggage handling but also unlimited carry-on space, window or aisle seats—even in coach class—and generous frequent-flyer bonuses.)
- Shortages of critical resources. (For example, a major retailer is unable to enter a geographical market because the pool of people historically interested in part-time work for "pocket money" has dried up; those individuals have gone to work in full-time professional jobs.)

Managers face an awesome challenge in this competitive and constantly changing environment, and this is not a passing phenomenon. As customer demands, global competition, and deregulation of industries in the United States and Europe increase, it has become clear that the current instability in our marketplaces is not going away. Change is and will continue to be the only constant.

The call to arms, chronicled in numerous books and articles, is widely understood by American businesspeople. Our concern is not managers' failure to understand the problem; it is their failure to do anything substantive to address the problem.

We wrote this book because we have a framework and a set of tools that can substantively address the problem. There are plenty of books on management and organization behavior. However, we find that most of them either fail to present tools (leaving the reader saying, "I'm a believer, but what do I do tomorrow?") or provide tools that address only one aspect of a multidimensional need. In our review of management literature, training courses, and consultant services, we have encountered some very valuable theories, hints, and tools. However, we have not come across a single organization performance improvement methodology that is conceptually sound, practical, experience-based, and comprehensive. We immodestly believe that our approach, based on Three Levels of Performance, meets these criteria and, by doing so, provides a blueprint for managing change.

Our second reason for writing this book is our desire to capture our forty years of combined experience in improving organization performance. We both started in the field of training (before it became human resource development [HRD]). Like many others, we were quick to realize that training is only one variable that affects human performance. During the late 1960s and early 1970s, we began learning about the environmental and managerial variables that influence performance. We then turned our attention to the impact of organization strategy on performance. During the 1980s, we developed a technology for documenting, improving, and managing the business processes that bridge the gap between organization strategy and the individual. With the evolution of Process Management, we believe we now have a comprehensive approach that addresses the major variables in the system that influence the quality, quantity, and cost of performance. Through the application of Process Management, we have learned that managers (particularly at senior levels) should concentrate as much or more on the flow of products, paper, and information *between* departments as on the activities *within* departments. Process Management provides a methodology for managing this white space between the boxes on the organization chart.

Purpose of the Book

The purpose of this book is to explain the underpinnings of our Three Levels framework and to demonstrate the tools through which the framework is applied and the white space can be managed. We have written it for performance improvement specialists (who may be professionals in human resource development, industrial engineering, quality, or systems analysis) and for line and staff managers who want to examine a process that can bring about significant performance improvement. We expect that performance improvement specialists will most often constitute the first wave of readers in an organization and that they will recommend all or part of the book to the managers who are their customers. In addition, business and organization behavior professors may find that our approach presents a different perspective.

American management has a tendency to manage by executive summary. A Director gets a one-page summary of an issue, a Vice President gets a paragraph, and the President gets a three-item list. At a recent conference on improving American manufacturing's ability to compete in the global market, one conferee criticized a session by saying, "If an idea can't be summarized in one page, it doesn't have any merit." We do not see how U.S. companies will ever best the Japanese with that view of executive information and analysis.

We are opposed to the "get it down to three items" school of management. Managers who are successful over the long haul understand their businesses in detail. As a result, the Three Levels approach has a fair amount of rigor. The approach is practical, involving a series of straightforward questions and steps. The process has been validated, through application to companies and agencies of all kinds. It can even be fun because teams improve the quality of work life, as well as product/service quality and productivity. But often it is not simple because the challenge is not simple. Any manager or performance improvement specialist who is looking for a quick-fix formula or for the latest program to keep employees stimulated is liable to be disappointed by this book.

Overview of the Chapters

Chapter One explores the forces driving the need to be more competitive. It suggests that the failure to meet the challenge has been due not to lack of desire or effort but to lack of understanding of the variables that influence organization and individual performance. Chapter Two contrasts the traditional functional view of the organization (as represented by the organization chart) with the more descriptive and useful systems view. The authors describe the system components that must be managed to establish an organization that is competitive, adaptive (reactively and proactively), and focused on continuous performance improvement.

The third chapter introduces the Three Levels of Performance and presents the nine Performance Variables that determine the effectiveness and efficiency of an organization. At each of Three Levels of Performance—the Organization Level, the Process Level, and the Job Level—this chapter describes the three Performance Needs—Goals, Design, and Management—and shows how they can be used by executives, managers, and analysts.

One of the Three Levels of Performance is explored in each of the next three chapters. Chapter Four provides a set of questions for diagnosing the effectiveness of the Goals, Design, and Management at the Organization Level. It illustrates the use of these questions in a sample company and presents the Relationship Map as a tool for understanding and improving performance at this level.

Chapter Five gives the reader tools for understanding and improving the goals, design, and management of the cross-functional processes through which an organization provides products and services to customers. This chapter continues the examination of the company introduced in Chapter Four and presents the Process Map as a methodology for meeting the needs at this Level of Performance.

Chapter Six uses the sample organization from Chapter Four to explore the role of people in improving organization and process performance. It presents the Human Performance System as a tool for understanding and meeting the Performance Needs (Goals, Design, and Management) of individuals and work teams.

The remaining chapters discuss the application of the systems view and the Three Levels framework to a variety of performance improvement opportunities faced by most North American corporations today. Chapter Seven examines the role of the systems view in ensuring that top management has answered all eleven questions that must be addressed to establish a clear, viable strategy. It goes on to show how the nine Performance Variables can help in implementing that strategy.

Through four examples, Chapter Eight shows how quality, productivity, cycle time, customer focus, and culture change efforts can fail if they do not address all Three Levels of Performance. It goes on to examine two performance improvement efforts that have benefited from covering all Three Levels.

Chapter Nine provides human resource, industrial engineering, and systems analysts with a comprehensive process for diagnosing organization Performance Needs before prescribing "solutions," such as training, reorganization, and developing management information systems. A case study illustrates each of the fourteen steps in this performance improvement process.

Chapter Ten describes the two-part methodology that companies such as IBM, GTE, Ford, and Motorola are using to improve quality and customer satisfaction and reduce cycle time and costs. Focusing on the pivotal Process Level of performance, Process Improvement helps document, analyze, and improve the performance of cross-functional processes, while Process Management establishes an infrastructure for ongoing process improvement.

Measuring performance and designing a performance management system is the focus of Chapter Eleven. This chapter addresses the "what," "why," and "how" of establishing a measurement system that encompasses all Three Levels of Performance. Examples illustrate establishing measures; developing a performance tracking system; and using measures as the basis for planning, feedback, performance improvement, and rewards.

Chapter Twelve presents a nine-step process for designing an organization structure that supports—rather than inhibits—the efficient delivery of high-quality products and services that meet customer needs. Using Relationship and Process Maps (introduced in Chapters Four and Five), a viable organization structure is developed for a sample company.

Chapter Thirteen uses a case example to demonstrate how the tools presented in Chapters Two through Twelve can be used to build an organization system that works and then to manage it as a system. Readers are given a set of questions for diagnosing the effectiveness of their organization systems, tools for holistically mapping the systems, and a description of the systems culture (versus the traditional hierarchical culture).

Chapter Fourteen draws on the authors' combined forty years of experience working with human resource development professionals and shows how the Three Levels approach can help these professionals make a more substantial contribution to organization performance. It describes how the Three Levels tools can help in needs analysis, training design, and evaluation and how they can transform the training operation into the organization's "Performance Department."

The final chapter describes a three-step process for getting started on a Three Levels project. It also provides examples of how the Three Levels tools have been unbundled and used to address specific issues and to help develop a customer-focused, participative, low-conflict, accountability-based culture.

Acknowledgments

We would like to acknowledge the individuals who have made this book possible. First, we thank our clients, who provided us with the real-world crucible in which our technology was developed. While our experience results from interactions with hundreds of people in dozens of organizations, we would like to offer special thanks to Ken Massey (Grupo Industrial ALFA), John Murphy (formerly of GTE and now of The Executive Edge), "Duke" Schmidt of Ford (now retired), Mal Warren (formerly of Questor and now of CVS), and Bill Wiggenhorn of Motorola.

Second, we thank our professional colleagues, from whom we have learned a great deal about performance: Dale Brethower, Karen Brethower-Schetky, George Geis, Tom Gilbert, Jaime Hermann, George Odiorne, and Carl Semmelroth.

Third, we thank the staff of The Rummler-Brache Group, who provided beyond-the-call-of-duty support to us as we pursued two full-time jobs—serving our clients and writing this book. Special thanks go to Sheri Bach, Larry Bataille, Traci Hilbert, Rick Rummler, and Ede Shanahan. We also thank Leonard and Zeace Nadler, Jossey-Bass consulting editors, who, we hope, have helped us communicate to a wider audience.

Finally, we offer special thanks to our families and friends, who encour-
aged and supported us throughout this effort.

April 1990   Geary A. Rummler
                                                          Tucson, Arizona

                                                          Alan P. Brache
                                                          Irving, Texas

THE AUTHORS

Geary A. Rummler is a partner in The Rummler-Brache Group, a research and consulting group specializing in the design and development of organization performance systems for business and governmental organizations in the United States and abroad. He received his B.A. degree (1959), his M.B.A. degree (1960), and his Ph.D. degree (1971) from the University of Michigan.

Prior to founding The Rummler-Brache Group, he served as President of the Kepner-Tregoe Strategy Group, specialists in strategic decision making. He cofounded and was President of Praxis Corporation, an innovator in the analysis and improvement of human performance, and cofounded and was Director of the University of Michigan's Center for Programmed Learning for Business.

Rummler was a pioneer in the application of instructional and performance technologies to organizations, and he brings this experience to the issue of organization effectiveness. His clients in the private sector have included the sales, service, and manufacturing functions of the aircraft, automobile, steel, food, rubber, office equipment, pharmaceutical, telecommunications, chemical, and petroleum industries, as well as the retail banking and airline industries. Rummler has also worked with such federal agencies as the Internal Revenue Service, the Social Security Administration, the Office of Housing and Urban Development, the General Accounting Office, and the Department of Transportation. His research and consulting have taken him to Europe, Japan, Korea, Malaysia, China, and Mexico.

Rummler has published a variety of books whose topics range from labor relations to the development of instructional systems, and his articles have appeared in numerous professional and management journals and handbooks. He is coauthor of *Training and Development: A Guide for Professionals* (1988, with G. S. Odiorne).

A member of the Training Research Forum, Rummler has also served as national president of the National Society for Performance and Instruction, as a member of the Research and Strategic Planning Committees of the American Society of Training and Development, and as a member of the editorial board of *Training* magazine. In 1986, he became the seventh inductee into the Human Resource Development Hall of Fame.

As a partner in The Rummler-Brache Group, **Alan P. Brache** shares with Geary A. Rummler responsibility for the strategy and operations of the firm. Brache's client work involves managing organization performance improvement projects that employ consulting and training solutions.

Much of his recent writing and client work has been in the area of Process Management, a tool for improving organization performance through the identification and removal of cross-functional barriers to effectiveness. He has recently been involved in quality-improvement efforts with companies in the aerospace and telecommunications industries.

Before joining The Rummler-Brache Group, Brache spent nine years with Kepner-Tregoe, Inc. He last served as Corporate Vice President and Director of Technical Services and Client Support in the Kepner-Tregoe Strategy Group. In that capacity, he was responsible for strategic product development, internal professional development, and the management of a group of consultants who delivered projects concerned with strategy formulation and strategy implementation. Much of his work involved helping his clients implement their strategies and equip their middle managers with strategic thinking skills. He designed and delivered the training for Kepner-Tregoe's own strategy consultants.

Prior to assuming this position, Brache was responsible for the development, introduction, customization, quality, and refinement of Kepner-Tregoe's training programs and consulting services in the areas of problem solving, decision making, performance management and appraisal, standard setting, productivity improvement, organization change, participation, and human resource development. He specialized in organization diagnosis, responding to nonstandard needs and helping clients integrate management techniques into organization systems.

Before joining Kepner-Tregoe, Brache spent four years as an employee development specialist for the Social Security Administration. His focus in this position was on consulting, course development, and instruction in the areas of problem solving, decision making, performance management, planning, and communication.

Brache has worked with small, medium, and large organizations in a variety of industries in twelve countries. He regularly addresses national and international management and human resource associations and conventions. His publications include articles in *Business, Management Review, Training and Development Journal, Supervisory Management Training, Government Executive, Quality Progress,* and *Management World.* He has also developed an audiotape series on managerial leadership.

IMPROVING PERFORMANCE

How to Manage
the White Space
on the Organization Chart

CHAPTER 1

INTRODUCTION: THE CHALLENGES FACING AMERICAN BUSINESS

There is nothing in this world constant, but inconstancy.
—Jonathan Swift

The pressures on American management have been well publicized: formidable global competition, increasingly demanding customers, dwindling natural and skilled human resources, quantum leaps in technology. The theme that unites these pressures is change—relentless, multifaceted, unforgiving, blindingly rapid change.

The message has gotten through. We don't believe that American managers need more "war stories" about dissatisfied customers, the Japanese industrial miracle, the impact of automation, or the dangers of focusing on quarterly results. We American managers are as aware as we need to be. Now, we need to do a better job of doing something about it. We need to face the challenge of change.

All too often, American companies respond to external pressure with spasmodic campaigns such as:

- Developing and communicating a business vision and/or strategy
- Embarking on culture-transformation programs
- Training executives in "leadership" (as opposed to "management," which is now widely seen as the domain of uninspiring, dime-a-dozen technocrats)
- Conducting organizationwide quality awareness and customer awareness campaigns, spearheaded by Directors of Quality
- Training employees in statistical process control tools
- Automating operations
- Downsizing and other forms of cost cutting (the goal of which is to become "lean and mean")
- Exhorting employees to strive for "excellence," "innovation," and "entrepreneurial risk taking"

If management's objective is to symbolize to employees, customers, share-holders, and the business press that it recognizes the challenge and is doing something about it, then any of these actions will do the job. If, however, managers wish to address needs comprehensively and on a sustained basis, they cannot pursue the quick fixes and superficial responses that have become the trademark of American improvement efforts.

Noble intentions drive each of the actions listed here, and each of them can address a piece of the problem or opportunity. Therein, however, lies our concern. Managing to meet the challenge of change — demanding, unforgiving customers and ubiquitous, unmerciful competitors — is a complex and complicated task. *Piecemeal approaches that are assumed to be* **the** *answer are as dangerous as no response at all.* These efforts can absorb vast resources as they lull an organization into thinking that it is addressing its needs.

Whether the concern is quality, customer focus, productivity, cycle time, or cost, the underlying issue is *performance*. In our opinion, most American managers have been unable to respond effectively to the challenges because they have failed to create an infrastructure for systemic and continuous improvement of performance. We believe that their shortcoming does not lie in the understanding of the problem, in the desire to address the problem, or in the willingness to dedicate resources to the resolution of the problem. Rather, *the majority of managers simply do not understand the variables that influence organization and individual performance.* They are not aware of the "performance levers" that they should be pulling and encouraging others to pull. If they are blind to these levers, it is most likely because they have a picture of their business that does not reflect the way work actually gets done.

American managers have been flagellated enough by pundits of organization behavior. While we agree with much of the criticism, we have no need to add our voices to the chorus. We can make a more significant contribution by sharing an approach that has demonstrated its ability to address the need. The remainder of this book describes the *Three Levels of Performance*.

- This approach is based on a world view that reflects the way work actually gets done in organizations.
- It addresses performance in a comprehensive (rather than piecemeal) fashion.
- It focuses on the Nine Variables that represent management's performance improvement levers.
- This approach presents tools, rather than a mere theory or model of performance.
- It demystifies the connection between human performance and organization performance.
- It has been used successfully by large, medium, and small organizations in manufacturing, service, and government.
- Finally, it provides a basis for optimism: the challenge can be met.

PART ONE:
A FRAMEWORK
FOR IMPROVING
PERFORMANCE

,,,

CHAPTER 2

VIEWING
ORGANIZATIONS
AS SYSTEMS

Adapt or die.

— Unknown

The Traditional (Vertical) View of an Organization

Many managers don't understand their businesses. Given the recent "back to basics" and "stick to the knitting" trend, they may understand their products and services. They may even understand their customers and their competition. However, *they often don't understand, at a sufficient level of detail, how their businesses get products developed, made, sold, and distributed.* We believe that the primary reason for this lack of understanding is that most managers (and nonmanagers) have a fundamentally flawed view of their organizations.

When we ask a manager to draw a picture of his or her business (be it an entire company, a business unit, or a department), we typically get something that looks like the traditional organization chart shown in Figure 2.1. While it may have more tiers of boxes and different labels, the picture inevitably shows the vertical reporting relationships of a series of functions.

As a picture of a business, what's missing from Figure 2.1? First of all, it does not show the customers. Second, we cannot see the products and services we provide to the customers. Third, we get no sense of the work flow through which we develop, produce, and deliver the product or service. Thus, Figure 2.1 doesn't show what we do, whom we do it for, or how we do it. Other than that, it's a great picture of a business. But, you may say, an organization chart isn't supposed to show those things. Fine. Where's the picture of the business that *does* show those things?

In small or new organizations, this vertical view is not a major problem because everybody in the organization knows each other and needs to understand other functions. However, as time passes and the organization

Figure 2.1. Traditional (Vertical) View of an Organization.

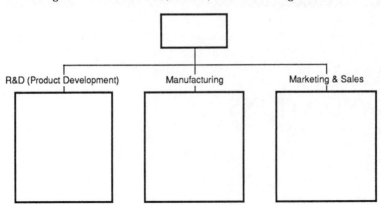

becomes more complex as the environment changes and as technology becomes more complicated, this view of the organization becomes a liability.

The danger lies in the fact that when managers see their organizations vertically and functionally (as in Figure 2.1), they tend to manage them vertically and functionally. More often than not, a manager of several units manages those units on a one-to-one basis. Goals are established for each function independently. Meetings between functions are limited to activity reports.

In this environment, subordinate managers tend to perceive other functions as enemies, rather than as partners in the battle against the competition. "Silos" (tall, thick, windowless structures, like those in Figure 2.2) are built around departments. These silos usually prevent interdepartmental issues from being resolved between peers at low and middle levels. A cross-functional issue around scheduling or accuracy, for example, is escalated to the top of a silo. The manager at that level addresses it with the manager at the top of the other silo. Both managers then communicate the resolution down to the level at which the work gets done.

The silo culture forces managers to resolve lower-level issues, taking their time away from higher-priority customer and competitor concerns. Lower-level employees, who could be resolving these issues, take less responsibility for results and perceive themselves as mere implementers and information providers. This scenario is not even the worst case. Often, function heads are so at odds that cross-functional issues don't get addressed at all. In this environment, one often hears of things "falling between the cracks" or "disappearing into a black hole."

As each function strives to meet its goals, it optimizes (gets better and better at "making its numbers"). However, *this functional optimization often contributes to the suboptimization of the organization as a whole.* For example, Marketing/Sales can achieve its goals and become a corporate hero by selling lots of products. If those products can't be designed or delivered on schedule

Figure 2.2. The "Silo" Phenomenon.

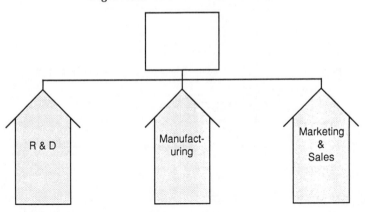

or at a profit, that's R&D's, Manufacturing's, or Distribution's problem; Marketing did its job. R&D can look good by designing technically sophisticated products. If they can't be sold, that's Marketing's problem. If they can't be made at a profit, that's Manufacturing's problem. Finally, Manufacturing can be a star if it meets its yield and scrap goals. If the proliferation of finished goods sends inventory costs through the roof, that's the concern of Distribution, or Marketing, or perhaps Finance. In each of these situations, a department excels against traditional measures and, in so doing, hurts the organization as a whole.

When the manager of functions A, B, and C goes to the manager of subfunction B to determine why B failed to produce on time, the response tends to be: "It's those so-and-so's in A." An interview with the CEO of General Motors in the August 24, 1987, issue of *Forbes* illustrates this phenomenon. *Forbes* asks why such reorganization is necessary:

> "Couldn't you just call in the boss of Fisher Body and say, 'If I get one more complaint about your division, you and the top three guys are finished'?"
>
> Without quite intending to, Roger Smith's answer says a lot about what went wrong with the corporate behemoth and why it responded so slowly. The sickness is called passing the buck.
>
> "Okay, we could do that, and it's the way we used to do it. But he [the Fisher man] says, 'Wait a minute. I did my job. My job was to fabricate a steel door, and I made a steel door, and I shipped it to GMAD. And it's GMAD's fault.' So you go over to the GMAD guy and say: 'Listen, one more lousy door and you're fired.' He says, 'Wait a minute, I took what Fisher gave me and the car division's specs and I put them together, so it's not my fault.'"
>
> "So, you get the Chevrolet guy, and you say, 'One more

Figure 2.3. Systems (Horizontal) View of an Organization.

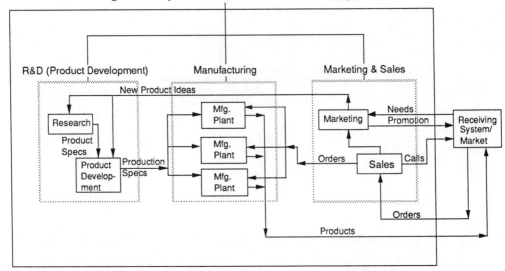

lousy door, and. . .' 'Wait a minute,' he says. 'All I got is what GMAD made.' So pretty soon you're back to the Fisher guy, and all you are doing is running around in great big circles."

Roger Smith's frustration illustrates how difficult it is for an organization with this strong "silo" orientation to effectively and efficiently respond to change.

In the good old days of a seller's market, it didn't matter. A company could introduce products at its own pace, meet only its own internal quality goals, and set prices that guaranteed adequate margins. There were no serious consequences to the evolution of functional silos like those illustrated in the examples. Those days are over. Today's reality requires most organizations to compete in a buyer's market. We need a different way to look at, think about, and manage organizations.

The Systems (Horizontal) View of an Organization

A different perspective is represented by the horizontal, or systems, view of an organization, illustrated in Figure 2.3. This high-level picture of a business:

- Includes the three ingredients missing from the organization chart depicted in Figure 2.1: the customer, the product, and the flow of work
- Enables us to see how work actually gets done, which is through processes that cut *across* functional boundaries

- Shows the internal customer-supplier relationships through which products and services are produced

In our experience, *the greatest opportunities for performance improvement
often lie in the functional interfaces — those points at which the baton (for example,
"production specs") is being passed from one department to another.* Examples of key
interfaces include the passing of new product ideas from Marketing to
Research and Development, the handoff of a new product from Research and
Development to Manufacturing, and the transfer of customer billing information from Sales to Finance. Critical interfaces (which occur in the "white
space" on an organization chart) are visible in the horizontal view of an
organization.

An organization chart has two purposes:

- It shows which people have been grouped together for operating
  efficiency.
- It shows reporting relationships.

For these purposes, the organization chart is a valuable administrative
convenience. However, it should not be confused with the "what," "why," and
"how" of the business; *all too often, it's the organization chart, not the business, that's
being managed.* Managers' failure to recognize the horizontal organization
explains their most common answer to the question "What do you do?" They
say (to refer to Figure 2.1), "I manage A, B, and C." Assuming that A, B, and C
already have competent managers, we have to ask if the senior manager sees
his or her job as remanaging those functions. If so, is that a role that justifies
his or her salary? We don't believe so. *A primary contribution of a manager (at the
second level or above) is to manage interfaces. The boxes already have managers; the
senior manager adds value by managing the white space between the boxes.*

In our experience, the systems view of an organization is the starting
point — the foundation — for designing and managing organizations that
respond effectively to the new reality of cutthroat competition and changing
customer expectations.

The Organization as an Adaptive System

Our framework is based on the premise that organizations behave as
adaptive systems. As Figure 2.4 shows, an organization is a processing system
(1) that converts various resource inputs (2) into product and service outputs
(3), which it provides to receiving systems, or markets (4). The organization is
guided by its own internal criteria and feedback (5) but is ultimately driven by
the feedback from its market (6). The competition (7) is also drawing on
those resources and providing its products and services to the market. This
entire business scenario is played out in the social, economic, and political

environment (8). Looking inside the organization, we see functions, or subsystems, which exist to convert the various inputs into products or services (9). These internal functions, or departments, have the same systems characteristics as the total organization. Finally, the organization has a control mechanism—management (10)—that interprets and reacts to the internal and external feedback, so that the organization keeps in balance with the external environment.

To illustrate the systems framework, let us examine a fictitious firm: Computec, Inc. As shown in Figure 2.5, Computec (1) is a software development and systems engineering firm. It takes in capital, staff, technology, and materials (2) and produces products and services (3), which include systems consulting services, custom software, and software packages. It sells its products and services to a primary market—aerospace companies—as well as to other industrial and individual markets. Computec has various internal mechanisms for checking the accuracy and efficiency of its coding, reports, and packages (5). Its customers give it feedback (6) through additional business, complaints, references, and requests for service. Its competitors (7) are

Figure 2.4. An Organization as an Adaptive System.

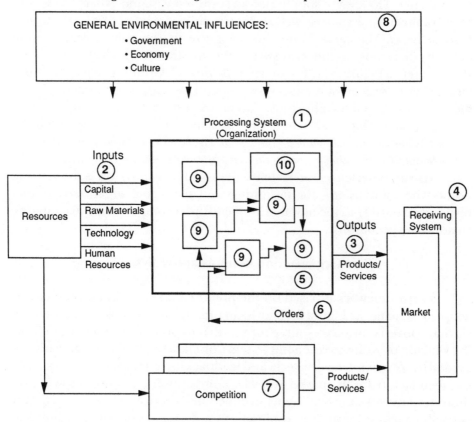

Figure 2.5. Computec, Inc., as an Adaptive System.

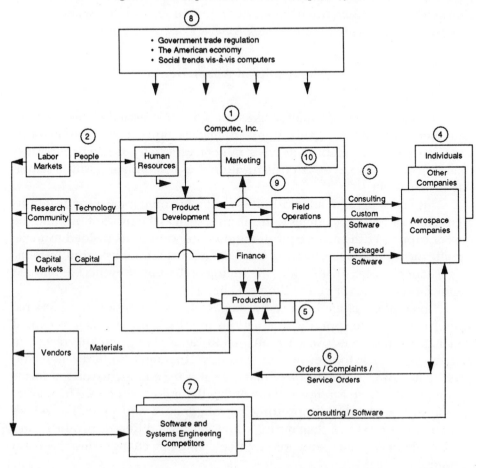

other software and systems engineering companies that serve Computec's markets. It conducts its business in the context of the American economic, social, and political environment (8). Inside Computec, such functions (9) as Marketing, Product Development, and Field Operations serve as internal suppliers and customers, which convert the company inputs into the company outputs. The management team (10) establishes the strategy, monitors the internal and external feedback, establishes goals, tracks performance, and allocates resources.

We contend that this systems perspective describes every organization. Even the systems of monopolies and government entities contain everything except the "competition" (7) component. The markets may change, products and services come and go, but the components of the system remain the same. In fact, the only thing we can say with certainty about the future of an organization (assuming it is still in business) is that the organization will operate in a system that includes the components of the model shown in

Figure 2.4. The potential evolution of a business is dramatically illustrated by Primerica, a diversified financial services company, which ten years ago was American Can, a typical "smokestack America" manufacturer.

The Reality of Adaptation

Primerica's transformation illustrates a fundamental element of systems theory applied to organizations—*adaptation*. A processing system (organization) will either adapt to its environment, especially its receiving system (market), or cease to exist. An organization seeks equilibrium with its external environment.

Fifteen years ago, adaptation was not a burning issue. Organizations adapted to significant changes in key inputs, such as the price of fuel and the cost of capital. With each major disruption, organizations needed to make significant adjustments. However, equilibrium was reestablished in months, or perhaps in a year. Historically, the timing of disruptive events has allowed organizations to adapt before the next change.

Today, the change is more fundamental, more frequent, and less patient. In addition to sporadic fluctuations in critical inputs, such as capital and natural resources, we have an ineradicable change in the receiving system—the marketplace—which seriously threatens both revenue and profit. The primary dimension of that change is the emergence of new forms of competition from foreign and deregulated domestic sources. The market has become destabilized, upsetting the oligopolies and perennial seller's market. Customers are demanding—and getting—different products and services, better quality, and lower prices, and the changes just keep on coming.

Systems laws and the free market enable and require organizations to adapt to these changing demands. If an organization survives, it has adapted. However, its health is a function of *how well* it has adapted. Eighteen months after Peters and Waterman (1982) published their list of "excellent" companies, one-third of them had dropped off the list. An examination of the fallen shows that the majority failed to respond adequately to changes in the external environment. Any set of criteria for excellence should include the ability to adapt. In our opinion, *the key variable in an organization's ability to effectively and speedily adapt is its management.*

What does a manager get out of the systems perspective? To the manager who doesn't take the systems view, the onslaught of change appears chaotic, unpredictable, and out of control. He or she sees a current crisis as a situation-specific event, rather than as part of a never ending need to adapt. *Adaptation is a process, not an event.* The systems framework in Figure 2.4 identifies the major generic forces of change and points up the need for continuous adaptation to these constantly changing forces. *An effective man-*

ager can use the systems framework in Figure 2.4 to predict and proactively cope with change.

Through "what if" scenarios around each of the components of the system, the rate and direction of change can be anticipated and built into the organization strategy. Say that we are the top management team in Computec. What will we do if a change in government (component 8) results in lower entry barriers to potential Japanese competitors? What if our two major competitors (component 7) merge? What personal computer products might the market (component 4) perceive to be substitutes for our minicomputer software? What computer hardware breakthroughs (component 2) could have a significant effect on our systems integration consulting services?

The rest of this book is dedicated to providing you with tools for analyzing the environments outside and inside your organization. Each of the tools is based on the systems view described here, and on the following fundamental laws of organizational systems:

1. Understanding performance requires documenting the inputs, processes, outputs, and customers that constitute a business. It is interesting to describe an organization as a culture, a set of power dynamics, or a personality. However, it is essential at some point to describe what it does and how it does it. (Chapters Four and Five provide tools for such a description.)

2. Organization systems adapt or die. The success of the survivors depends on the effectiveness and speed with which they adapt to changes in the external environment (customers' needs, competitors' actions, economic fluctuations) and in their internal operations (rising costs, inefficiencies, product development opportunities).

3. When one component of an organization system optimizes, the organization often suboptimizes. (Examples of this law have already been cited.)

4. Pulling any lever in the system will have an effect on other parts of the system. You can't just reorganize, or just train, or just automate, as if you were merely adding some spice to the stew. Each of these actions changes the recipe. (See the discussion of the Three Levels of Performance, Chapter Three.)

5. An organization behaves as a system, regardless of whether it is being managed as a system. If an organization is not being managed as a system, it is not being effectively managed. (Managing organizations as systems is the subject of Chapter Thirteen.)

6. If you pit a good performer against a bad system, the system will win almost every time. We spend too much of our time "fixing" people who are not broken, and not enough time fixing organization systems that are broken. (Chapter Six is devoted to managing the Human Performance Systems in which people work.)

We are performance improvement practitioners. We find the "organizations as systems" model useful because it enables us and our clients to understand the variables that influence performance and to adjust the variables so that performance is improved on a sustained basis. Chapter Three explores the variables—the management levers—that influence each of the Three Levels of Performance.

THREE LEVELS
OF PERFORMANCE:
ORGANIZATION, PROCESS,
AND JOB/PERFORMER

> *When we try to pick out anything by itself, we find it hitched to*
> *everything else in the universe.*
>
> *—John Muir*

Nineteenth-century environmentalist John Muir found that each component of the ecosystem is in some way connected to all other components. The 1981 brouhaha over the snail darter, which ultimately halted construction on the Clinch River breeder reactor, was not just about a tiny fish that affects very few of us; it was about tampering with a small tile in the environmental mosaic. Each tile that is removed or changed alters, if only in a minute way, the balance of the picture.

Similarly, we have found that everything in an organization's internal and external "ecosystem" (customers, products and services, reward systems, technology, organization structure, and so on) is connected. To improve organization and individual performance, we need to understand these connections. The current mosaic may not present a very pretty picture, but it *is* a picture. The picture can be changed or enhanced only through a holistic approach that recognizes the interdependence of the Performance Variables. We have found that the way to understand these variables is through the application of the systems view (described in Chapter Two) to Three Levels of Performance.

I: The Organization Level

When we take our first, macro "systems" look at the organization, we see the fundamental view and variables discussed in Chapter Two. This level—the *Organization Level*—emphasizes the organization's relationship with its market and the basic "skeleton" of the major functions that comprise the organization. Variables at Level I that affect performance include strategies,

organizationwide goals and measures, organization structure, and deploy-
ment of resources (see Figure 3.1).

II: The Process Level

The next set of critical variables affecting an organization's performance is at what we call the *Process Level.* If we were to put our organization
"body" under a special X ray, we would see both the skeleton of Level I and the
musculature of the cross-functional processes that make up Level II (see
Figure 3.2).

When we look beyond the functional boundaries that make up the

Figure 3.1. The Organization Level of Performance.

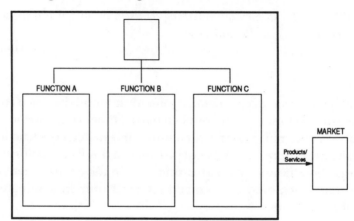

Figure 3.2. The Process Level of Performance.

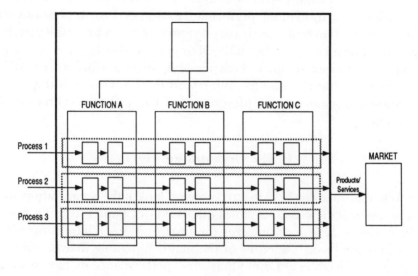

Figure 3.3. The Job/Performer Level of Performance.

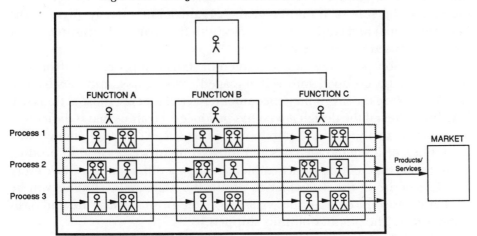

organization chart, we can see the work flow—how the work gets done. We contend that organizations produce their outputs through myriad cross-functional work processes, such as the new-product design process, the merchandising process, the production process, the sales process, the distribution process, and the billing process (to name a very few).

An organization is only as good as its processes. To manage the Performance Variables at the Process Level, one must ensure that processes are installed to meet customer needs, that those processes work effectively and efficiently, and that the process goals and measures are driven by the customers' and the organization's requirements.

III: The Job/Performer Level

Organization outputs are produced through processes. Processes, in turn, are performed and managed by individuals doing various jobs. If we increase the power of our X ray, as in Figure 3.3, we can see this third Level of Performance, which represents the cells of the body. The Performance Variables that must be managed at the Job/Performer Level include hiring and promotion, job responsibilities and standards, feedback, rewards, and training.

Now we have an organization X ray, which depicts the three critical interdependent Levels of Performance. The overall performance of an organization (how well it meets the expectations of its customers) is the result of goals, structures, and management actions at all Three Levels. If a customer receives a shipment of faulty framuses, for example, the cause may lie in any or all of the Three Levels. The *performer* may have assembled the framuses incorrectly and/or let faulty framuses be shipped. The *processes* that influence framus quality (including design, procurement, production, and distribution) may be at fault. The *organization*—represented by top managers who determine the role of framuses in the organization strategy, provide the budgets for staff and equipment, and establish the goals and measures—may also have caused the problem.

Assembly *performers* can be trained in statistical process control techniques, can be grouped into self-managed work teams, and can be empowered to stop the line if they encounter defects. However, those actions will have little effect if the design *process* has produced a framus that is difficult to assemble correctly, or if the purchasing process can't acquire enough subassemblies, or if out-of-sync sales and forecasting processes lead to product changeovers that require the assembler to follow a different procedure every day. The desire of the assembler to produce a high-quality framus will be further compromised if, in this *organization*, the primary measure and basis of rewards is "the number of units shipped."

The Three Levels represents an anatomy of performance. The anatomy of the human body includes a skeletal system, a muscular system, and a central nervous system. Since all of these systems are critical and interdependent, a failure in one subsystem affects the ability of the body to perform effectively. Just as an understanding of human anatomy is fundamental to a doctor's diagnosis and treatment of ailments in a body, an understanding of the Three Levels of Performance is fundamental to a manager's or analyst's diagnosis and treatment of ailments in an organization.

However, our focus is not only on curing such ailments. *Just as enlightened members of the medical community use their knowledge of human anatomy to promote wellness and preventive medicine, enlightened members of the management community use their knowledge of performance anatomy to prevent organization problems and continuously improve performance.* But they can't do it alone. These managers use the talents of their human resource, systems, and management analysts in the same way that veteran doctors benefit from the contributions of their interns, nurses, and laboratory staff.

In Chapter Eight, we describe four performance improvement efforts that are flawed by their failure to address one or more of the Three Levels of Performance. We present two examples of organizations that have successfully implemented improvement efforts, which included action at all Three Levels.

The Nine Performance Variables

The Three Levels of Performance constitute one dimension of our framework. The second dimension comprises three factors—*Performance Needs*—that determine effectiveness at each level (and the effectiveness of any system):

Table 3.1. The Nine Performance Variables.

THE THREE PERFORMANCE NEEDS

		Goals	Design	Management
THE THREE LEVELS OF PERFORMANCE	Organization Level	Organization Goals	Organization Design	Organization Management
	Process Level	Process Goals	Process Design	Process Management
	Job/Performer Level	Job/Performer Goals	Job Design	Job / Performer Management

1. *Goals*: the Organization, Process, and Job/Performer Levels each need specific standards that reflect customers' expectations for product and service quality, quantity, timeliness, and cost.
2. *Design*: the structure of the Organization, Process, and Job/Performer Levels needs to include the necessary components, configured in a way that enables the goals to be efficiently met.
3. *Management*: each of the Three Levels requires management practices that ensure that goals are current and are being achieved.

Combining the Three Levels with the Performance Needs results in the nine *Performance Variables*. These Variables, which appear in Table 3.1, represent a comprehensive set of improvement levers that can be used by managers at any level.

To illustrate the Three Levels approach, let's take a brief look at the company that we introduced in Chapter Two. To refresh your memory, Computec, Inc., is a software development and systems engineering firm, with 70 percent of its business from custom software development and consulting services. The other 30 percent of revenues is generated by off-the-shelf software packages.

Computec was successful for the first thirteen years of its existence. However, during the last two years, it has experienced significant erosion of its market share. Internal problems include high turnover and sinking morale. Senior management is concerned about the situation and has recently studied the organization culture and completed programs on organization renewal, total quality, and entrepreneurship. The next program is slated to be on customer focus. So far, company performance has not improved.

Realizing that previous medication may or may not have attacked the disease, we begin by diagnosing Computec. We will use the nine Performance Variables that make up the framework of the Three Levels approach.

Organization Level

Before we can effectively analyze the human dimensions of performance, we need to establish a macro-level context. At the Organization Level, we examine the nature and direction of the business and the way it is set up and managed. (In Chapter Four, we will present the specific tools; the following is a discussion of the three Performance Variables at the Organization Level.)

Organization Goals. At the Organization Level, goals are part of the business strategy. All Three Levels and all of the other Performance Variables build on the direction established by the Organization Goals. In this example, our primary question is whether Computec has established clear companywide goals that reflect decisions regarding (1) the organization's competitive advantage(s), (2) new services and new markets, (3) the emphasis it will place on its various products or services and markets, and (4) the resources it is prepared to invest in its operations and the return it expects to realize on these investments. Through this line of questioning, we find that Computec has not established a clear strategy.

Because the company dominated its historic market niche (aerospace project management) until two years ago, top management never spent much time investigating strategic alternatives and preparing for the current competitive environment. The executive team has recently realized the need for a strategy and a set of companywide goals derived from that strategy. While the executives have much more work to do in this area, they have established three clear goals: to aggressively develop new products and services, to provide a level of customer support that differentiates Computec from its competition, and to eliminate the company's competitive disadvantage in the quality and timeliness of filling its orders for standard software products. While these goals are not yet measurable, they provide guidance to employees who otherwise might think that Computec is banking on growth from its existing products, does not intend to feature customer service, and intends to emphasize price (rather than quality and timeliness) as its competitive advantage.

Organization Design. This variable focuses on the structure of the organization. We are certainly interested in the organization chart, but our systems view of performance makes us more interested in understanding how the work gets done and whether it makes sense. We would begin by developing a Relationship Map, which shows the interfaces among the Computec functions. (The Computec organization chart and Relationship Map appear in Chapter Four.)

We have two key questions: Does Computec have all of the functional components it needs to achieve its strategy? Should any input-output connections (supplier-customer relationships) be added, eliminated, or altered?

Although Computec has occasionally introduced new services, few have been successful. The company relies on two packaged software products and three services, all of which it developed early in its history. The organization structure does not support speedy, effective new-product development and introduction, postsale customer support, or order processing. Given Computec's Organization Goals, the organization structure will have to be realigned to support these three areas of strategic emphasis.

Organization Management. An organization may have appropriate goals and a structure that enables it to function as an efficient system. However, to operate effectively and efficiently, the organization must be managed. At the Organization Level, management includes:

- *Goal Management*: Involves creating functional subgoals that support the achievement of the overall organization goals. Failure to set goals that reflect a function's expected contribution to the entire organization will lead to the silo-based suboptimization discussed earlier.
- *Performance Management*: Involves obtaining regular customer feedback, tracking actual performance along the measurement dimensions established in the goals, feeding back performance information to relevant subsystems, taking corrective action if performance is off target, and resetting goals so that the organization is continually adapting to external and internal reality.
- *Resource Management*: Involves balancing the allocation of people, equipment, and budget across the system. Resource allocation should enable each function to achieve its goals, thereby making its expected contribution to the overall performance of the organization.
- *Interface Management*: Involves ensuring that the "white space" between functions is managed. In this capacity, managers resolve functional "turf" conflicts and establish infrastructures to support the collaboration that characterizes efficient, effective internal customer-supplier relationships.

The Organization Management question is this: Is the Computec executive team managing goals, performance, resources, and interfaces? Computec is not doing well in this area. Many of its functional goals are in conflict and support short-term profit, rather than the strategic goals around product development, customer service, and order processing. The company has no system for performance tracking, feedback, and improvement. Resources are allocated on a "whoever shouts loudest" basis, and the silos around Product Development, Marketing, and Operations are tall and well fortified. All four Organization Management areas will have to be addressed if Computec's strategy is to succeed.

Process Level

When we lift the lid and peer inside an organization, the first things we see are the various functions. However, the systems view suggests that this perspective does not enable us to understand the way work actually gets done, which is a necessary precursor to performance improvement. For this understanding, we need to look at *processes*. Most key dimensions of organization performance result from cross-functional processes, such as order handling, billing, procurement, product development, customer service, and sales forecasting. Chapter Five more fully explores the Process Level; the following is an overview of its three Variables, using Computec as an example.

Process Goals. Since processes are the vehicle through which work gets produced, we need to set goals for processes. The goals for processes that touch the external customer (for example, sales, service and billing) should be derived from the Organization Goals and other customer requirements. The goals for internal processes (for example, planning, budgeting, and recruiting) should be driven by the needs of the internal customers. (In Chapters Five and Eleven, we discuss process-oriented goal setting in more depth.)

Functional goals, which are part of the Organization Management variable just discussed, should not be finalized until we see the contribution that each function needs to make to the key processes. *Each function exists to serve the needs of one or more internal or external customers. If a function serves external customers, it should be measured on the degree to which its products and services meet those customers' needs. If a function serves only internal customers, it should be measured on the way it meets those customers' needs and on the value it ultimately adds to the external customer. In both cases, the key links to the customer are the processes to which the function contributes.*

The installation process, for example, is critical to any company that installs equipment in a business or a residence. One function that contributes to the installation *process* is the Sales Department. Even though Sales may not be part of the installation itself, it is part of the installation process because salespeople usually write orders that include specifications for equipment installations. Because it has a significant impact on the quality and timeliness of an installation, the Sales Department should be measured on the accuracy, specificity, understandability, and timeliness with which its people provide installation specifications to the department that performs the installation. Installation specification goals are not necessarily part of the Sales measurement system. However, when you look at the organization as a set of processes, and at the Sales Department in terms of the contributions it makes to all the processes it supports, a richer set of goals emerges.

For our overview of Computec's performance in terms of Process Goals, we have two primary questions: Does the company have goals for its processes (particularly those cross-functional processes that influence the strategy)? Are the Process Goals linked to customers' requirements and to the Organization Goals?

Given Computec's strategic thrusts and vulnerabilities, its key processes are the product/service development process, the customer support process, and the order-filling process (for its off-the-shelf software). Not surprisingly, Computec has no goals for these processes. Furthermore, its functional goals do not support the optimal performance of these processes.

Process Design. Once we have Process Goals, we need to make sure that our processes are structured (designed) to meet the goals efficiently. Processes should be logical, streamlined paths to the achievement of the goals. As part of our Computec analysis, we have one simple question that addresses this variable: Do the company's key processes consist of steps that enable it to meet Process Goals efficiently?

Earlier, we determined that Computec has no Process Goals. However, we can still examine its three key processes. The mechanism for product development and introduction is not really a process, by anyone's definition of the term. Products and services eventually emerge from poorly coordinated projects, which are characterized by functional bickering, budget overruns, missed deadlines, and lack of ownership. When the order-filling process is analyzed, the only surprise is that Computec does occasionally meet customers' expectations for quality and timeliness. A customer support process has never really been created. This company has a lot of work to do in the process area. (Examples of Computec processes appear in Chapter Five.)

Process Management. A process with a logical structure will be ineffective if it is not managed. Process Management includes the same ingredients as Organization Management:

- *Goal Management*: Involves establishing subgoals at each critical process step. These goals should drive functional goals.
- *Performance Management*: This involves regularly obtaining customer feedback on the process outputs, tracking process performance along the dimensions established in the goals, feeding back performance information, identifying and correcting process deficiencies, and resetting process goals to reflect the current customer requirements and internal constraints.
- *Resource Management*: Involves supporting each process step with the equipment, staff, and budget it needs to achieve its goals and make its expected contribution to the overall Process Goals.
- *Interface Management*: Involves managing the "white space" between process steps, especially those that pass between functions. As at the Organization Level, where the greatest opportunities for improvement lie be-

tween functions, the greatest process improvement opportunities often lie between process steps.

Does Computec manage the goals, performance, resources, and interfaces of its key processes? Since Computec has not established a crossfunctional orientation to its business, it has not established a Process Management infrastructure for its key processes. (Since Process Management is so critical to performance improvement and has so many nuances, Chapter Ten is entirely devoted to that subject.)

Job/Performer Level

The Organization and Process Levels may be beautifully wired in terms of goals, design, and management. However, the electricity will flow only if we address the needs of the people who make or break organization and process performance. If processes are the vehicle through which an organization produces its outputs, people are the vehicle through which processes function. (We address the human dimension of performance through the Job Level, which is covered in depth in Chapter Six.)

Job/Performer Goals. Just as we need to establish Process Goals that support Organization Goals, we need to establish goals for the people in those jobs that support the processes. In examining Computec, we ask what jobs contribute to each key business process, and whether the outputs and standards (goals) of these jobs are linked to the requirements of the key business processes (which are in turn linked to customer and organization requirements).

One of Computec's key processes is the off-the-shelf software order-filling process. A variety of jobs in the Sales, Production, and Finance functions contribute to this process. Like most companies, Computec is not doing a good job of goal setting at the Job Level. The Job Goals that have been set have not been tied to process requirements. Computec needs to establish process-driven goals for each job in the functions just listed. If the company does not take this step, the odds of achieving the strategic (Organization Level) goals are low.

Job Design. We need to design jobs so that they make the optimum contribution to the Job Goals. The Job Design question is a simple one: Has Computec structured the boundaries and responsibilities of its jobs so that they enable the Job Goals to be met? Again, Computec has never looked at its business through the eyes of Organization, Process, and Job Goals, and so it has never used that perspective as the basis for structuring jobs.

Job/Performer Management. The list of ingredients in Job Management does not fall into the goals/performance/resources/interfaces categories we used when discussing the variables of Organization Management and Process Management. Job Management is really people management. However, this definition supports managers' tendency to overmanage individuals and undermanage the environment in which they work. Therefore, Job Management is more accurately defined as managing the Human Performance System.

While it may sound as if this approach dehumanizes the management of people, the effect is quite the contrary. Human Performance System management is based on the premise that people, for the most part, are motivated and talented. If they don't perform optimally, the cause is most likely in the system (at the Organization, Process, and/or Job Level) in which they've been asked to perform. The Human Performance System, like the organization system, is composed of inputs, processes, outputs, and feedback, all of which need to be managed.

If Computec is effectively managing the Human Performance System of its key jobs, the managers and incumbents in those jobs would answer yes to these questions:

- *Performance Specifications*: Do the performers understand the outputs they are expected to produce and the standards they are expected to meet? (This question relates to Job Goals.)
- *Task Interference*: Do the performers have sufficient resources, clear signals and priorities, and a logical set of job responsibilities? (The last part of this question relates to Job Design.)
- *Consequences*: Are the performers rewarded for achieving the Job Goals?
- *Feedback*: Do the performers know whether they are meeting the Job Goals?
- *Skills and Knowledge*: Do the performers have the necessary skills and knowledge to achieve the Job Goals?
- *Individual Capacity*: In an environment in which the five questions listed above were answered affirmatively, would the performers have the physical, mental, and emotional capacity to achieve the Job Goals?

If Computec is to be successful, its managers must create a supportive environment around the people who will determine whether the company strategy becomes reality. For example, one of Computec's Organization Goals is to improve its customer service to the point at which it becomes a competitive advantage. Its customer service hotline is currently staffed on a rotating basis by Field Operations people, who consider phone duty punishing, believe it takes them away from their real jobs, and do not have the skills to handle customers' complaints effectively and efficiently. If customer service is to be a competitive advantage, needs related to Task Interference, Consequences, and Skills and Knowledge will have to be addressed.

A Holistic View of Performance

Table 3.2 shows the questions associated with each of the nine performance variables in our framework. This systems view of performance has led us to two conclusions:

- Effective management of performance requires goal setting, structuring, and managing each of the Three Levels of Performance — the Organization Level, the Process Level, and the Job/Performer Level.
- The Three Levels are interdependent. For example, a job cannot be properly defined by someone who doesn't understand the requirements of the business process(es) that the job exists to support. Any attempt to implement Organization Goals will fail if those goals are not supported by processes and Human Performance Systems.

The Three Levels framework provides some insight into the shortcomings of many attempts to change and improve organizations. For example:

- Most training attempts to improve organization and process performance by addressing only one Level (the Job Level) and only one dimension of the Job Level (skills and knowledge). As a result, the training has no significant long-term impact, training dollars are wasted, and trainees are frustrated and confused.
- Automation is generally an attempt to improve the performance of the Process Level. However, the investment in automation rarely realizes its maximum return because the link is not made between the process and the Organization Goals to which it is intended to contribute: the process is inefficient, and so the result is an automated inefficient process; and the automation fails to consider the needs of the Human Performance Systems of the people involved in the process.
- If programs to improve performance in such areas as quality, productivity, and customer focus are just hype, they don't address the needs of any of the Three Levels. Programs that establish Organization Goals and train employees usually fail to address the needs at the Process Level and the goals, feedback, and consequences required at the Job Level.

Using the Three Levels Framework

This framework (summarized in Table 3.2) as well as the process and tools that it has spawned, has evolved over twenty years of research and

Table 3.2. The Nine Performance Variables with Questions.

Performance Needs

Performance Levels	GOALS	DESIGN	MANAGEMENT
ORGANIZATION LEVEL	**ORGANIZATION GOALS** • Has the organization's strategy/direction been articulated and communicated? • Does this strategy make sense, in terms of the external threats and opportunities and the internal strengths and weaknesses? • Given this strategy, have the required outputs of the organization and the level of performance expected from each output been determined and communicated?	**ORGANIZATION DESIGN** • Are all relevant functions in place? • Are there unnecessary functions? • Is the current flow of inputs and outputs between functions appropriate? • Does the formal organization structure support the strategy and enhance the efficiency of the system?	**ORGANIZATION MANAGEMENT** • Have appropriate function goals been set? • Is relevant performance measured? • Are resources appropriately allocated? • Are the interfaces between functions being managed?
PROCESS LEVEL	**PROCESS GOALS** • Are goals for key processes linked to customer/organization requirements?	**PROCESS DESIGN** • Is this the most efficient/effective process for accomplishing the Process Goals?	**PROCESS MANAGEMENT** • Have appropriate process sub-goals been set? • Is process performance managed? • Are sufficient resources allocated to each process? • Are the interfaces between process steps being managed?
JOB / PERFORMER LEVEL	**JOB / PERFORMER GOALS** • Are job outputs and standards linked to process requirements (which are in turn linked to customer and organization requirements?)	**JOB DESIGN** • Are process requirements reflected in the appropriate jobs? • Are job steps in a logical sequence? • Have supportive policies and procedures been developed? • Is the job environment ergonomically sound?	**JOB / PERFORMER MANAGEMENT** • Do the performers understand the Job Goals (outputs they are expected to produce and the standards they are expected to meet)? • Do the performers have sufficient resources, clear signals and priorities, and a logical job design? • Are the performers rewarded for achieving the Job Goals? • Do the performers know if they are meeting the Job Goals? • Do the performers have the necessary knowledge/ skill to achieve the Job Goals? • If the performers were in an environment in which the five questions listed above were answered "yes," would they have the physical, mental, and emotional capacity to achieve the Job Goals?

application in companies, agencies, divisions, departments, functions, and stores. It has been used as:

- A *tool* for diagnosing and eliminating deficient performance (for example, excessive semi-conductor chip manufacturing and delivery cycle time; loss of margins in a retail chain)
- An *engine* for continuously improving systems that are performing adequately (for example, increasing responsiveness to airlines' needs for unique aircraft configurations; increasing timeliness of telecommunications customer service)
- A *road map* for guiding an organization in a new direction (for example, toward entering the software business or selling in a newly deregulated environment)
- A *blueprint* for designing a new entity (for example, an electronics "factory of the future"; a marketing department in a public utility)

The Three Levels framework has proved valuable to:

- *Executives*, who provide the vision, leadership, and impetus for change
- *Managers* at all levels, who implement companywide changes by providing vision and leadership on the Organization Level for the departments they manage
- *Analysts*, who design the systems and procedures that enable managers to implement the change

For all three of these forces of change to work efficiently in concert, they must have the same objectives and process. The Three Levels of Performance has been designed to meet this need. The remainder of this book addresses the performance improvement responsibilities of all three roles.

PART TWO:
EXPLORING
THE THREE LEVELS
OF PERFORMANCE

CHAPTER 4

THE ORGANIZATION LEVEL OF PERFORMANCE

All are but parts of one stupendous whole.

—Alexander Pope

A wealthy owner of a baseball franchise will often recruit the most highly skilled (and highly priced) talent and wonder why his or her team doesn't win the World Series. A championship team often pales in position-to-position matchups; it wins because somehow the "stupendous whole" is greater than the sum of its parts. The distinction is usually that the winning team as a whole, not just each individual player and function (hitting, pitching, defense), is being managed.

Similarly, an organization can be greater than the sum of its parts only if the whole organization is managed. An organization may have people with outstanding experiential and academic credentials. Its functions, such as marketing, production, and research, may look good when benchmarked against those departments in other organizations. However, its results may be less than stellar because its executives manage functions and people without placing them in a larger organizational context. This practice is a prescription for suboptimization, a situation in which the whole equals less than the sum of its parts. Our first step in managing organization performance— Level I of the Three Levels—is to acknowledge the viewpoints that often characterize the current situation.

The Customer's View of the Organization. "What is going on with these people? Why can't they give me a product that does what I need it to do and is available when I need it? Where is the follow-up service I was told I'd be getting? Why do I feel that I know more about the product than they do? Why do I have to deal with a different person each time I contact them? Why can't these people get their act together?"

The Supplier's View of the Organization. "Why don't these people ever know what parts they need more than three days ahead of time? Do they realize that because we have to expedite nearly every order, they end up paying top dollar? Why do they keep changing the specifications? Why do they discontinue at least one product every six months, which results in a large number of part returns? Why don't they ever take us up on our offer to visit their plant, at our expense, so we can learn what's happening in their business? Why can't these people get their act together?"

The Employees' View of the Organization. "Why can we match our competitor's quality only by dramatically increasing inspection (which drives our costs through the roof)? Who told Sales that we have the capability to offer that service and meet that deadline? Where do the Product Development people come up with these ideas? So, what are our priorities *this* week? Why don't Section Managers cooperate with each other? Don't these people realize that if we don't change the way we do business, we won't survive? How does top management expect us to believe that quality comes first when, at the end of every month, they say 'I don't care; ship it!'? Why are these people, who are paid above the industry average, still not motivated? Why can't we get our act together?"

Exploring the Organization Level

Before we can effectively address the bleak but all too common situations just depicted, we have to understand them. The best way we have found for understanding how an organization functions is to see the organizations as an adaptive system. This view, which is described in depth in Chapter Two (see Figure 2.4, p. 10), maintains that every organization operates as a processing system, which converts inputs (such as resources and customer orders) into outputs (products and services) that it provides to its customers. The organization continuously adapts in order to maintain equilibrium with its environment, which includes its market, its competition, its resource pool, and the socioeconomic context in which it functions. As we discussed in Chapter Two, an organization that adapts nimbly is likely to succeed; an organization that adapts lethargically is likely to fail.

The systems view does not apply only to an entire company or agency. If we look inside an organization, we see that it is made up of layer upon layer of systems. As Figure 4.1 illustrates, one of the systems in an automobile company is its manufacturing system. One of manufacturing's components is its production system. Production is made up of a number of systems, one of

Figure 4.1. Layers of Organization Systems in an Automobile Company.

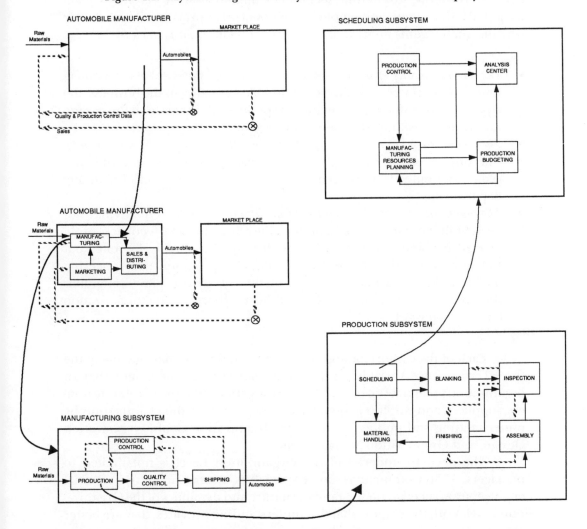

which is scheduling. By peeling the organization like an onion, in this manner, we have found that we can understand how it operates, as well as the variables affecting its performance, at any level of detail.

Understanding and Managing the Organization Level

If executives do not manage performance at the Organization Level, the best they can expect is modest performance improvement. At worst, efforts at other levels will be counterproductive. We have observed a number of companies in which quality improvement is a major thrust. They have embraced statistical process control tools, just-in-time techniques, manufacturing resources planning (MRP II) systems, and employee empowerment practices. They wonder why the quality gains aren't more dramatic. Inevitably, it is because:

- *The various quality efforts are not driven by a clear statement of organization strategy.* The strategy should define the role of quality in the business, the types of quality that represent the competitive advantage, and the organizationwide, customer-driven measures of quality.
- *The organization has not been designed in a way that supports maximum quality.* The impact of the noble efforts in training, tools, systems, and procedures is limited by the organization structure and relationships among departments.
- *The organization is not managed with quality as the driver.* Quality has not been built into tactical goals, performance tracking and feedback, problem solving, and resource allocation. And quality is typically rolled out function by function (there is a design quality program, an engineering quality program, a manufacturing quality program). The tremendous threats and opportunities within the "white space" on the organization chart are ignored.

Each of these shortcomings represents a failure to manage one of the three Performance Variables at the Organization Level. We believe that an organization's managers can "get their act together" (the plea of the customers, suppliers, and employees quoted at the beginning of this chapter) only by understanding and pulling the levers of Organization Goals, Organization Design, and Organization Management.

The need to understand the Organization Level is not limited to managers. Analysts (human resource specialists, systems analysts, industrial engineers) also need to understand the nature and dynamics of the Organization Level. With the context that this understanding provides, they are better able to design improvements that have the maximum positive impact on the performance of their organizations.

The Performance Variables at the Organization Level

Organization Goals. At the Organization Level, goals are strategic. A good strategy identifies the organization's:

- Products and services
- Customer groups (markets)
- Competitive advantage(s)
- Product and market priorities (emphasis areas)

Organization Goals, therefore, are stated in terms of how well products and services are expected to do in the various markets to which they are offered. An effective set of Organization Goals includes:

- The values of the organization
- Customers' requirements
- Financial and nonfinancial expectations
- Targets for each product family and market
- Expectations for each competitive advantage to be established or enhanced

Procedurally, Organization Goals should be:

- Based on the critical success factors for the company's industry
- Derived from competitive and environmental scanning information
- Derived from benchmarking information (intelligence on the performance of systems and functions in exemplary organizations)
- Quantifiable whenever possible
- Clear to all who have to understand and be guided by them

Organization Goals for Computec, Inc., the organization we introduced in Chapter Two, might include:

- *Never sacrifice quality for short-term net income.*
- *Increase the company's customer satisfaction rating to 98 percent by the end of the year.*
- *Introduce three new software products and two new systems integration services within two years.*
- *Capture 60 percent of the aerospace project management market within three years.*
- *By the end of the year, introduce two new customer services that differentiate Computec from its competitors.*
- *Reduce software package order cycle time to an average of seventy-two hours by the end of next year.*
- *By the end of next year, fill orders with 100 percent accuracy.*

These Organization Goals are quantitative, customer-oriented, competitive advantage–driven, and easily understood. With these and other goals as a context, Computec can embark on performance improvement efforts in the areas of quality, productivity, total cycle time, and cost control. These Organization Goals will serve as the high-level measures of the success of these efforts.

Most important, the Computec Organization Goals are clearly derived from its strategy. They reflect the executives' tough choices regarding products, markets, competitive advantages, and priorities. (To help identify those tough choices, we have developed a detailed set of questions that need to be answered in applying the systems view and the Three Levels of Performance to strategy development and implementation; those questions are included in Chapter Seven.)

In summary, these are the questions for the Organization Goals:

- Has the organization's strategy/direction been articulated and communicated?
- Does this strategy make sense in terms of external threats and opportunities and internal strengths and weaknesses?
- Given this strategy, have the required outputs of the organization and the level of performance expected from each output been determined and communicated?

Since this is our first discussion of goals, it is probably a good place to take a stand. Some of the followers of quality-and-productivity guru W. Edwards Deming are avidly against goal setting. They believe that goal achievement leads to complacency, which serves as a barrier to continuous improvement. That can happen. However, we believe that goals should be continually evaluated and reset to fit changing requirements and capabilities. If goals are adapted in this way, they can support rather than hinder the noble pursuit of continuous improvement. (Please note that reestablishment of goals is one of the key steps in Performance Management, which is discussed later in this chapter.)

Organization Design. Unfortunately, establishing clear Organization Goals is only the first step. Managers and analysts need to design an organization that enables the Goals to be met. To find out if the existing organization supports the achievement of the Organization Goals, we develop a Relationship Map. As the name indicates, the purpose of this picture of the business is to depict the customer-supplier relationships among the line and staff functions that make up the business. Because the Relationship Map makes visible the inputs and outputs that flow among functions, it shows what is going on in the "white space" between the boxes on the organization chart. Figure 4.2 contains a traditional organization chart for Computec. Figure 4.3 displays a Computec Relationship Map.

We use the Relationship Map to:

- Understand how work currently gets done (how the organization behaves as a system)
- Identify "disconnects in the organization wiring" (missing, unneeded, confusing, or misdirected inputs or outputs)
- Develop functional relationships that eliminate the disconnects

Figure 4.2. Computec, Inc., Organization Chart.

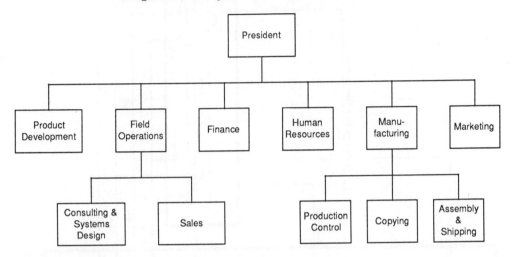

- Evaluate alternative ways to group people and establish reporting hierarchies

Our initial approach to Organization Design, therefore, is to examine and improve the input-output relationships among functions. To us, the structure depicted by the Relationship Map is most important because that's the structure through which work gets done. *When the focus is placed on the internal and external customer-supplier relationships, the standard organization chart becomes less important.* However, the reporting hierarchy can facilitate or impede the flow of work. (We have devoted Chapter Twelve to a discussion of an organization structure that works. In that chapter, we address the need for the vertical and horizontal systems to peacefully coexist.)

In summary, these are the questions that underlie the variable of Organization Design:

- Are all relevant functions in place?
- Are there unnecessary functions?
- Is the current flow of inputs and outputs between functions appropriate?
- Does the formal organization structure support the strategy and enhance the efficiency of the system?

Figure 4.3. Relationship Map for Computec, Inc.

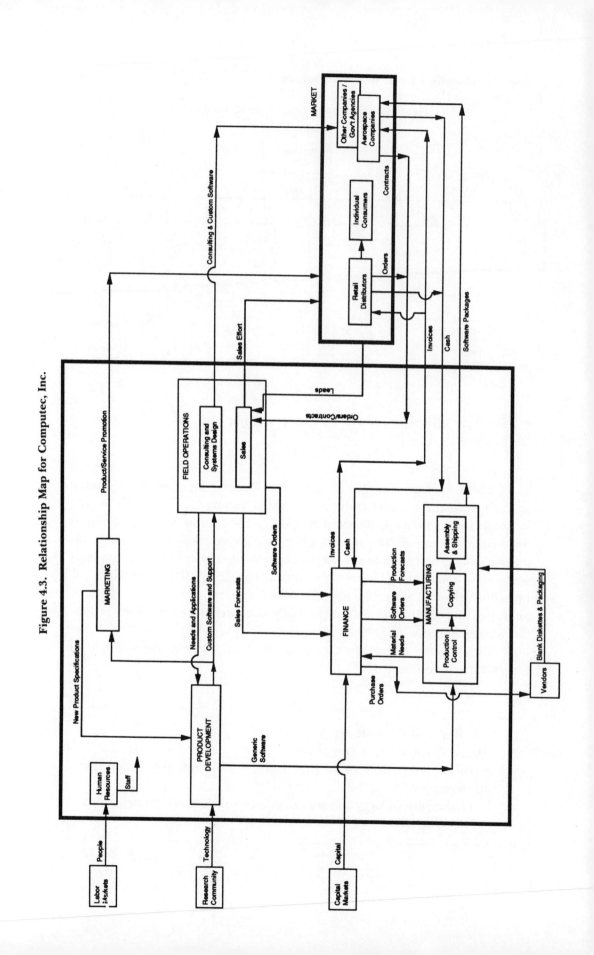

An examination of Computec's Relationship Map reveals a number of Organization Design disconnects that could hamper the company's ability to achieve its Organization Goals. These disconnects include:

- Marketing does not participate in sales forecasting.
- Marketing is not linked to Field Operations.
- Marketing does not identify needs through market research.
- No function provides customer service.
- Diskette orders have to go through both Sales and Finance before they go to Production to be filled.
- Production forecasts are done by Finance.

Unfortunately, identifying disconnects doesn't make them disappear. Computec needs to design an organization that will eliminate the disconnects that are hampering its ability to achieve Organization Goals. (Chapter Twelve discusses the use of the systems view and the Relationship Map to structure an organization. In addition to providing examples of structuring an organization to remove disconnects, Chapter Twelve shows how mapping and derivative tools can be used to support a new strategy, to create a new enterprise or function, and to implement systemic improvements, such as automation and staff reduction. Chapter Thirteen addresses the need to manage the structure that has been created.)

Organization Management. Once the Organization Goals and Organization Structure have been established, the organization needs to be managed. Managing the organization—the horizontal organization—as a system includes four dimensions:

1. *Goal Management*: Each function needs to have subgoals, which support the achievement of the Organization Goals. As we discussed in Chapter Two, an effective set of subgoals does not permit the optimization of the functional silos and the suboptimization of the system as a whole. If each Computec function is to make its maximum contribution to the company as a whole, it will need to be measured against goals that are derived from its strategy (Organization Goals) and that help other functions achieve their goals. For example, Computec's Product Development department should have goals that:

- *Reflect the Organization Goal of ambitious and speedy new product and service development*
- *Ensure that its new products and services are driven by the needs of the marketplace, not by technical wizardry*
- *Require it to design products and services that Marketing can sell*
- *Require it to design products and services that Field Operations and Production*

can sell, make, and deliver with the quality and timeliness required by customers and the profit required by Computec.

2. *Performance Management*: To achieve the goals, performance needs to be managed at the Organization Level. To continue the Computec product development example, Computec senior management needs to:

- *Obtain regular feedback on product effectiveness from Computec's customers*
- *Measure Product Development, Marketing, and Field Operations on their contributions to the Organization Goal of product development and introduction*
- *Provide feedback to Product Development, Marketing, and Field Operations on their product development and product introduction performance*
- *Ensure that cross-functional problem-solving teams address product development and product introduction problems*
- *Reestablish product development and product introduction goals if there is a change in the market*

Peeling back one layer of the organizational onion, the management of Product Development needs to:

- *Regularly obtain feedback on product effectiveness from Computec's customers and from Product Development's internal customers — Marketing and Field Operations*
- *Measure performance in terms of the goals it has established (Product Development will **get** performance in the areas in which it **measures** performance)*
- *Feed back performance information to the subunits within Product Development*
- *Solve problems that impede its progress toward the function's goals*
- *Reestablish goals to fit the current reality of its internal and external markets*

3. *Resource Management*: Computec Product Development has two resource needs: sufficient people and dollars to meet its goals, and allocation of its resources to those areas of Product Development that will enable the goals to be met. As with Performance Management, this places responsibility on both the senior management of Computec and the management of Product Development. If the executive committee members want to reduce costs, they would be foolish to mandate a 10 percent personnel reduction in all departments. They should realize that cutting 10 percent of the Product Development staff may very well compromise one of Computec's key Organization Goals; perhaps headcounts should not be reduced at all in Product Development and should be reduced by 20 percent in another department. Since Organization Goals will be achieved only through the horizontal organization, top management must allocate resources across the entire horizontal organization. Peeling back one layer of the onion, the Vice President of Product Development is responsible for allocating resources across the horizontal organization that exists within his or her department.

4. *Interface Management*: If the senior managers of Computec take the systems view of performance, they will realize that key barriers to and opportunities for Organization Goal achievement reside in the "white space" between functions. They will realize that the product introduction goal will be achieved only if the product development and product introduction system (which includes the functions of Marketing, Product Development, and Field Operations) works well. The top team (ideally, aided by a Relationship Map) should be clear on the inputs and outputs that flow among these three functions and should spend a significant amount of time ensuring that this flow—this set of interfaces—is smooth.

The Vice President of Product Development has the same responsibility: to ensure that the various subcomponents within that department are effectively and efficiently working together.

In summary, these are the questions for Organization Management:

- Have appropriate functional goals been set?
- Is relevant performance measured?
- Are resources appropriately allocated?
- Are the interfaces between functions being managed?

Summary

If the Organization Level of performance is not being defined, designed, and managed, there is no context for or driver of human and system performance. In this environment, well-intentioned activities are carried out in a vacuum and are frequently off the mark. Considerations related to the Organization Level are important to any organizational unit, from an entire company or agency to the smallest subdepartment. Variables and tools concerned with the Organization Level can be used by:

- *Executives*, to understand how the business operates, to refine the organization strategy and measures, to establish appropriate departmental relationships, to create a workable organization structure, and to manage the interfaces among departments
- *Managers*, to understand how their businesses operate and how they fit into the big picture, to establish department goals, to strengthen relationships with other departments, to create a workable organization structure, and to manage the interfaces among subunits within their departments
- *Analysts*, to understand how their client organizations currently operate and how they measure results, to identify areas where their efforts will have the greatest payoffs, to determine the impact of system changes and

other proposed improvements on the organization as a whole, and to recommend enhancements that will have a positive effect on organizationwide performance

By answering questions such as those listed for each of the three variables at the Organization Level, and by using tools such as the Relationship Map, one can guide organization performance and bring it under control. This chapter begins with a bleak scenario involving customers, suppliers, and employees. Effective management of the Organization Level can go a long way toward converting those viewpoints.

The Customer's View of the Organization. "These people are highly responsive to our needs. They frequently know what we want and need before we do. While their product is good, what keeps us coming back is the after-sale service. They don't promise what they can't deliver. We have established a solid, long-term relationship with our Account Executive. We're proud to have them as a vendor."

The Supplier's View of the Organization. "These people appear to know where they're going. They give us plenty of lead time when they need parts for a new or modified product. They enforce especially tight specifications on those dimensions of our parts that contribute to their competitive edges. And they include us in the process of developing their competitive edges. Because they treat us as a business partner, we'll go the extra mile for them. We're proud to be their vendor."

The Employees' View of the Organization. "Everyone in this organization takes responsibility for doing the job right the first time. We can't afford any mistakes. Before they promise a modified product or a nonstandard delivery schedule to a customer, Sales talks to Product Development, Manufacturing, and Distribution. I can reach fairly quick agreement with other departments because we all understand the interdependencies and the priorities necessary to keep our customers coming back. Products are developed by a team composed of Marketing, Manufacturing, and Product Development. Meetings are frequently attended by customers and prospects. Every employee knows the strategy of the company and how his or her goals contribute to that strategy. I understand my priorities. When they change, I know why. People realize that their role is to serve the needs of internal or external customers. Section Managers know that they will not achieve their goals if they don't cooperate with the sections that serve as their suppliers and customers. I am motivated by the challenge provided by my job and by the support I am given. I realize that I am a critical link in the chain. I'm proud to work here."

Utopia? Not in our experience. These prevailing views are the natural result of an organization that "has its act together" at each of the Three Levels of Performance, and it all starts at the Organization Level. The Performance Variables and Tools at the Organization Level help identify what needs to get done (goals), the relationships necessary to get it done (design), and the practices that remove the impediments to getting it done (management). With an effective Organization Level as a foundation, we can begin to understand, analyze, and manage performance at the Process and Job/Performer Levels, which are covered in the next two chapters.

CHAPTER 5

THE PROCESS LEVEL
OF PERFORMANCE

Looking out upon the future, I do not view the process with any misgivings. I could not stop it if I wished; no one can stop it. Like the Mississippi, it just keeps rolling along.
— *Winston Churchill*

We have found the Process Level to be the least understood and least managed level of performance. Processes are rolling along (or, frequently, stumbling along) in organizations, whether we attend to them or not. We have two choices — we can ignore processes and hope that they do what we wish, or we can understand them and manage them. We have proposed (Chapter Two) that the only way to truly understand the way work gets done is to view an organization horizontally (as a system), rather than vertically (as a hierarchy of functions). When you view an organization horizontally, you see business processes.

In Chapter Four, we discussed the systems view at the Organization Level. We introduced the Relationship Map as a tool for viewing an organization as a system. We showed how a tremendous amount of learning and eventual improvement can result from the documentation and examination of the input-output (customer-supplier) linkages depicted in a Relationship Map.

However, between every input and every output is a *process*. Our understanding and improvement are incomplete if we don't peel the onion and examine the processes through which inputs are converted to outputs. While the Organization Level provides a perspective, sets a direction, and points to areas of threat and opportunity, our experience strongly suggests that the Process Level is where the most substantive change usually needs to take place. A clear strategy and logical reporting relationships (Organization Level) and skilled, reinforced people (Job/Performer Level) cannot compensate for flawed business and management processes.

What Is a Process?

A business process is a series of steps designed to produce a product or service. Some processes (such as the programming process) may be contained wholly within a function. However, most processes (such as order processing) are cross-functional, spanning the "white space" between the boxes on the organization chart.

Some processes result in a product or service that is received by an organization's external customer. We call those *customer processes*. Other processes produce products that are invisible to the external customer but essential to the effective management of the business. We call those *administrative processes*. Examples of these types of business processes appear in Table 5.1. Another category of processes—*management processes*—includes actions managers should take to support the business processes. Management processes include goal setting, day-to-day planning, performance feedback, rewards, and resource allocation. (Examples of management processes are included in Chapter Eleven and Chapter Thirteen.)

A process can be seen as a "value chain." By its contribution to the creation or delivery of a product or service, each step in a process should add value to the preceding steps. For example, one step in the product development process may be "prototype market-tested." This step adds value by ensuring that the product is appealing to the market before the design is finalized.

At the Organization Level, we "peel the onion" to increase our understanding of the customer-supplier relationships among functions. At the Process Level, we peel the onion by breaking processes into subprocesses. The manufacturing process, for example, may comprise these subprocesses: scheduling, tooling, fabrication, assembly, and testing.

Why Look at Processes?

An organization is only as effective as its processes. Organization Goals (see Chapter Four) can be achieved only through logical business processes, such as those listed in Table 5.1. For example, one of an automobile manufacturer's Organization Goals may be to reduce the time it takes to deliver a car with the options requested by a customer. The company cannot hope to meet this goal if it has an inefficient ordering process or a convoluted distribution process.

When we view the situation from the top down, we see that process effectiveness is a major variable in the achievement of Organization Goals. We can also look at the value of processes from the bottom up. At the Job/Performer Level, we can take a variety of steps to improve performance (see Chapter Six). For example, we can improve our recruiting and promotion practices. We can provide more specific, up-to-date job descriptions, more effective tools, and more attractive incentives. We can drive decision making down in the organization. We can empower teams to solve problems in their

Table 5.1. Examples of Business Processes.

Generic Customer Processes

- Marketing and sales
- Product/service development and introduction
- Manufacturing
- Distribution
- Billing
- Order processing
- Customer service
- Warranty administration

Industry-Specific Customer Processes

- Loan processing (banking)
- Claim adjudication (insurance)
- Grant allocation (government)
- Merchandise return (retail)
- Food preparation (restaurant)
- Baggage handling (airline)
- Operator services (telecommunications)
- User-manual writing (computer)
- Reservation handling (hotel)

Generic Administrative Processes

- Formal strategic and tactical planning
- Budgeting
- Recruiting
- Training
- Facilities management
- Purchasing
- Information management

work units. However, *even talented and motivated people can improve organization performance only as much as the business processes allow.*

To continue our automobile distribution example, salespeople may be thoroughly completing order forms, data-entry clerks may be accurately coding information, and dock crews may be efficiently loading cars onto trucks. However, the effectiveness of any improvement in their performance could be limited by the logic (or illogic) of the total distribution process, made up of the order entry, production scheduling, and transportation subprocesses.

People in jobs such as these can certainly influence the effectiveness and efficiency of the processes to which they contribute. However, we have found that individual and team problem solving rarely focuses on process improvement. Furthermore, actions taken in a single organizational unit often lead to the reinforcement of the functional silos and the system suboptimization discussed in Chapter Two. *The net message is that, over the long haul, strong people cannot compensate for a weak process. All too often, management relies on individual or team heroics to overcome fundamentally flawed processes.* Why not *fix* the processes and enlist our heroes in the battle against the competition.

Finally, the Process Level is important because *process effectiveness and efficiency should drive a multitude of business decisions. For example, a reorganization serves no purpose if it doesn't improve process performance. Jobs should be designed so that people can best contribute to process outputs. Automation is a waste of money if it calcifies an illogical process.* The pivotal link between organization performance and individual performance can be established only through the three variables at the Process Level — Process Goals, Process Design, and Process Management.

The Performance Variables at the Process Level

Process Goals. Each customer process and each administrative process exists to make a contribution to one or more Organization Goals. Therefore, each process should be measured against Process Goals that reflect the contribution that the process is expected to make to one or more Organization Goals. In our experience, most processes do not have goals. While functions (departments) usually have goals, most key processes cross functional boundaries. If we are working in an organization in which billing is a key process, and if we ask for the goals of the billing process, the response usually is "Oh, you mean the goals of the Billing Department." When we reply that we really do mean the billing *process* — including those steps accomplished outside the Billing Department — we frequently get blank stares.

We believe that measurement is most effective if it is done in relation to targets, or goals. Process Goals are derived from three sources: Organization Goals, customers' requirements, and benchmarking information. Process benchmarking — comparing a process to the same process in an exemplary organization — is particularly useful. Often the organization that is best in its class for a given process is not a competitor and is therefore easy to study. Organizations have learned a lot by benchmarking their order-handling and distribution processes to those of L. L. Bean, their product development processes to those of 3M, and their customer service processes to those of IBM.

One of the Organization Goals of Computec, Inc., our software and systems engineering company (see Chapter Four), is to introduce three new software products and two new system integration services within two years. As a result, Computec's product development and product introduction process is critical to its strategic success. The goals it might establish for this process include:

- *We will introduce our first new software product within nine months, our second within eighteen months, and our third within twenty-four months.*
- *We will introduce two new system integration services within twelve months.*

- *Our five new products and services will generate a total of $4.4 million in revenues and $660,000 in profits during the first full year after their introduction.*
- *The aerospace industry's need for each new product or service will be supported by current market research.*
- *Each new product and service will have applications outside as well as within the aerospace industry.*
- *New products and services will be unique or will be superior (in the eyes of the customer) to competitors' offerings.*
- *New products and services will use our existing sales and delivery systems.*

These Process Goals are linked both to Organization Goals and to customers' requirements. Note that they are not merely goals for the Product Development department. These Process Goals also reflect the performance expected of Product Development's partners in the process of product development and introduction—Marketing, Sales, and Field Operations. By meeting these goals, this process will make a significant contribution to the realization of the company's strategic vision.

A second Computec Organization Goal is to reduce the software package's order cycle to an average of seventy-two hours by the end of next year. For this Goal, Computec's order-filling process becomes strategically critical. The Goals for this process might include:

- No products will be shipped to incorrect addresses because of Computec's errors.
- We will meet our seventy-two-hour goal without increasing the cost of order filling.
- We will provide our customers with a single point of contact for order questions and feedback.

Given Computec's Organization Goals, its managers should also establish Process Goals for the customer support process. (The impact of Process Goals on functions will be discussed in the section on Process Management.) In all cases, the key question for Process Goals is:

- Are goals for key processes linked to customer and organization requirements?

Process Design. Once Computec has established goals for its critical processes, its managers need to ensure that the processes are designed to achieve those goals efficiently. To determine whether each process and subprocess is appropriately structured, we recommend that a cross-functional team build a Process Map, which displays the way work currently gets done. While the Relationship Map, which is built at the Organization Level (see Chapter Four), shows input-output relationships among departments, a Process Map documents, in sequence, the steps that the departments go through to convert inputs to outputs for a specific process. *All too often, a team finds that there isn't an established process; the work just somehow gets done.*

Figure 5.1 contains an "is" (current state) Process Map of Computec's order-filling process, as developed by a team representing all functions that contribute to the process. The mapping process starts by identifying the functions, departments, or disciplines involved with the process, listing them on the left-hand axis, and drawing a horizontal band for each. Once this is done, the team (made up of representatives from all the functions listed — possibly including the customer) traces the process of converting the input (orders) through all the intervening steps until the final required output (payment) is produced. The map shows how all functions are involved as the order is processed. This mapping format allows the team to see all the critical interfaces, overlay the time to complete various subprocesses on the map, and identify "disconnects" (illogical, missing, or extraneous steps) in the process.

As the Computec team documented and analyzed the current process for filling an order, it identified a number of disconnects.

- Sales Reps take too long to enter orders.
- There are too many entry and logging steps.
- Sales Administration slows down the process by batch-processing orders.
- Credit checking is done for both old and new customers.
- Credit checking holds up the process because it is done before (rather than concurrently with) order picking.

The team then created a "should" Process Map, which reflects a disconnect-free order-filling process. That Map appears in Figure 5.2.

As the figure shows, the major changes in the "should" map are:

- Direct order entry by Sales, eliminating Sales Administration
- Parallel order processing and credit checking
- Elimination of multiple order-entry and order-logging steps

Another possible "should" process would include a just-in-time production system, in which packages are assembled to order and not inventoried.

Is and Should Process Mapping are the central steps in process im-

Figure 5.1. Computec Order Filling: An "Is" Process Map.

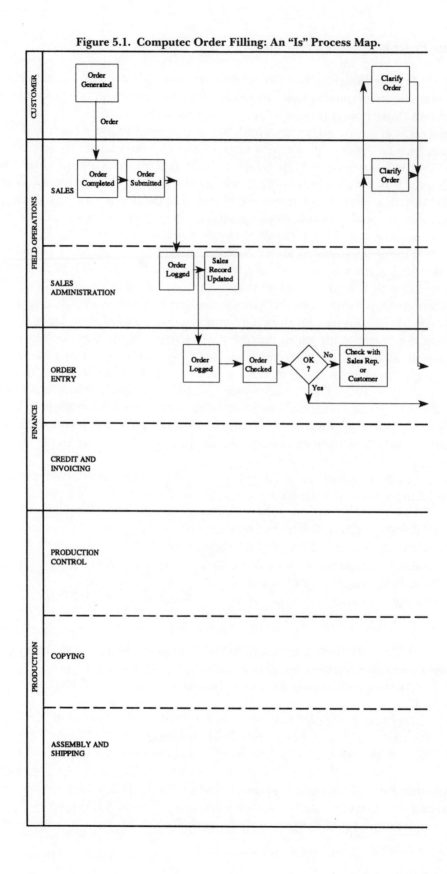

Figure 5.1. Computec Order Filling: An "Is" Process Map, Cont'd.

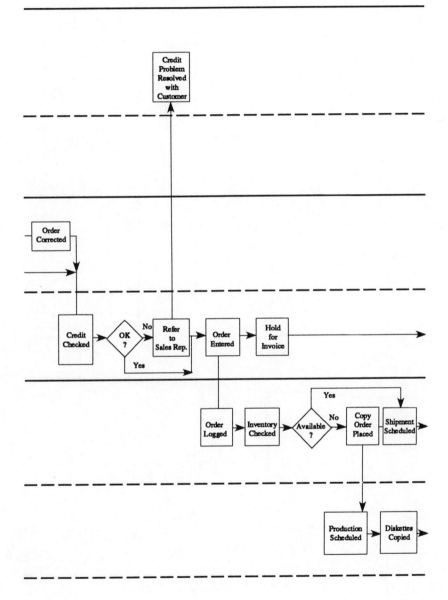

Figure 5.1. Computec Order Filling: An "Is" Process Map, Cont'd.

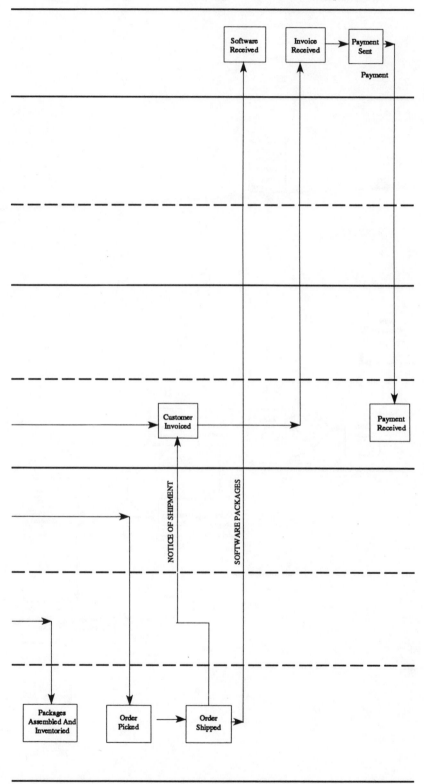

provement projects. (A complete list of process improvement project steps appears in Chapter Ten.) A successful process improvement project results in an affirmative answer to the key Process Design question:

> • Is this the most efficient and effective process for accomplishing the Process Goals?

Process Management. Unfortunately, even the most logical, goal-directed processes don't manage themselves. These are the four components of effective Process Management:

1. *Goal Management:* The overall Process Goals should serve as the basis for the establishment of subgoals throughout the process. If we managed a natural-gas pipeline, we would want to measure pressure and purity, not only at the end but also at various critical junctures along the line. Similarly, we need to establish process subgoals after each step that has an especially critical impact on the ultimate customer-driven Process Goals. Figure 5.3 shows some examples of process subgoals for Computec's order-filling process.

Many organizations, particularly in manufacturing industries, use Statistical Process Control (SPC) tools. We fully support the use of these tools, such as control charts, to track process performance, reveal problems, and maintain process stability. We have found that the goal-setting approach depicted in Figure 5.3 helps identify *where* SPC tools should be used.

Once process subgoals have been established, functional goals can be developed. Any functional goals established at the Organization Level should be modified, if necessary, to reflect maximum functional contributions to the Process Goals and subgoals. *Since the purpose of a function is to support processes, it should be measured on the degree to which it serves those processes. When we establish functional goals that bolster processes, we ensure that each department meets the needs of its internal and external customers.*

Computec's first step should be to identify each function's contribution to the process. For example, order entry is the first segment (subprocess) of the order-filling process. Three functions contribute to this segment:

- Sales, which enters the order via telephone
- Finance, which determines the customer's credit status
- Production Control, which determines the inventory status and, if necessary, triggers copying to produce additional diskettes

One way to summarize this contribution is through a Role/Responsibility Matrix, an example of which is included in Chapter Eleven.

On the basis of these contributions, and on the basis of the process

Figure 5.2. Computec Order Filling: A "Should" Process Map.

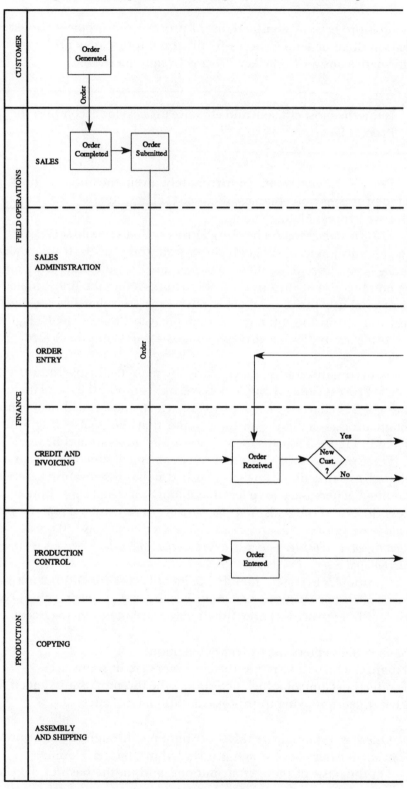

Figure 5.2. Computec Order Filling: A "Should" Process Map, Cont'd.

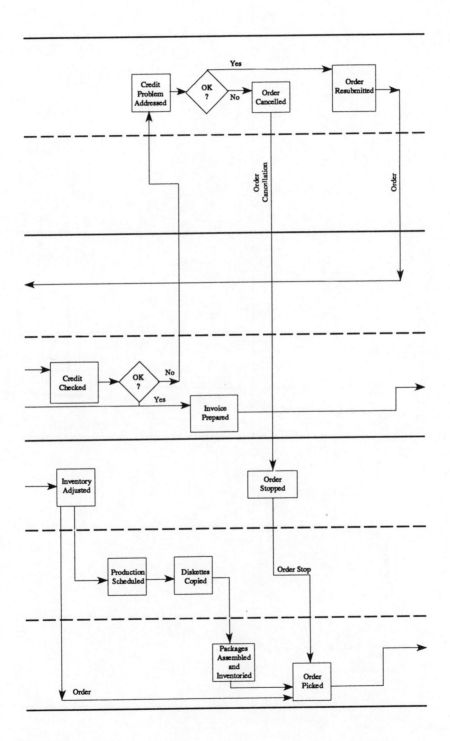

Figure 5.2. Computec Order Filling: A "Should" Process Map, Cont'd.

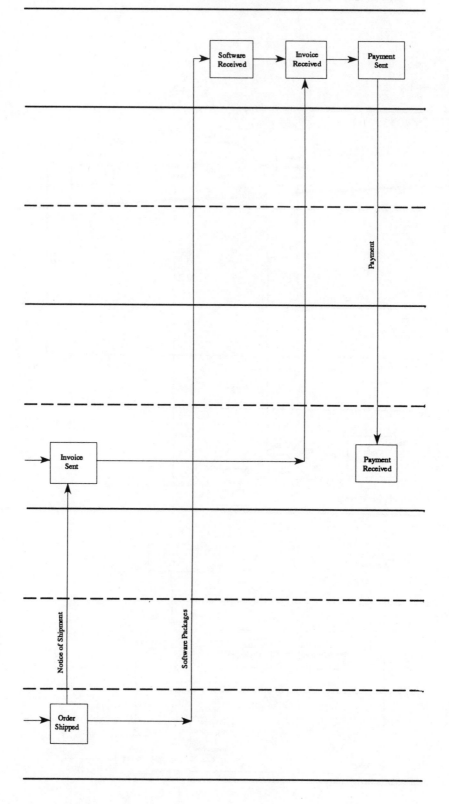

subgoals displayed in Figure 5.3, Computec should establish functional goals, such as those that appear in Table 5.2.

2. *Performance Management.* After Computec has established a workable order-filling process (Figure 5.2) and a set of goals and subgoals for its performance (Process Goals and Figure 5.3), its managers should establish systems for obtaining internal and external customer feedback on the process outputs, tracking process performance against the goals and subgoals, feeding back process performance information to the functions that play a role, establishing mechanisms to solve process problems and continuously improve process performance, and adjusting goals to meet new customer requirements. (In Chapter Eleven, we provide an example of a Performance Tracker that could be used to capture process performance information.)

During the last few years, we have learned a lot about managing process performance (which is, in effect, managing the horizontal organization). We have learned that if processes are to be managed on an ongoing basis (and not just fixed when they break), then managers must establish an infrastructure, which many organizations are beginning to call *Process Management*.

Computec senior managers could take several Process Management actions to ensure that the order-filling process is continuously managed:

- Rate the performance of the process, giving it a grade in such areas as customer satisfaction, cost, clarity and thoroughness of documentation, and quality and quantity of measures. Each function's contribution to the process could also be rated.
- Designate a Process Owner to oversee the entire process. (The criteria for selecting Process Owners and a description of their possible roles are included in Chapter Ten.)
- Identify a permanent process team, which would meet monthly to review and improve process performance.
- Hold monthly operations reviews, in which process performance would be reviewed first and function performance would be reviewed second.
- Reward people within a function only if Process Goals were met *and* if the function's contribution goals were met.

Process Management is such a pivotal theme within the Three Levels of Performance that we have devoted all of Chapter Ten to that subject.

3. *Resource Management*: Managers have always understood that resource allocation is a major part of their responsibility. However, process-focused resource allocation tends to be different from the usual function-oriented approach. Functional resource allocation usually results from a series of one-to-one meetings between a senior manager and his or her departmental or subdepartmental managers. In these meetings, each manager makes a case for a bigger slice of the pie, and the most persuasive

Figure 5.3. Selected Process Subgoals for Computec's Order-Filling Process.

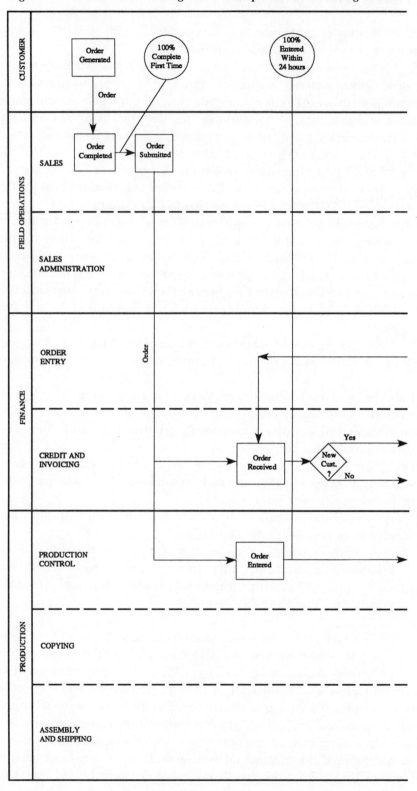

Figure 5.3. Selected Process Subgoals for Computec's Order-Filling Process, Cont'd.

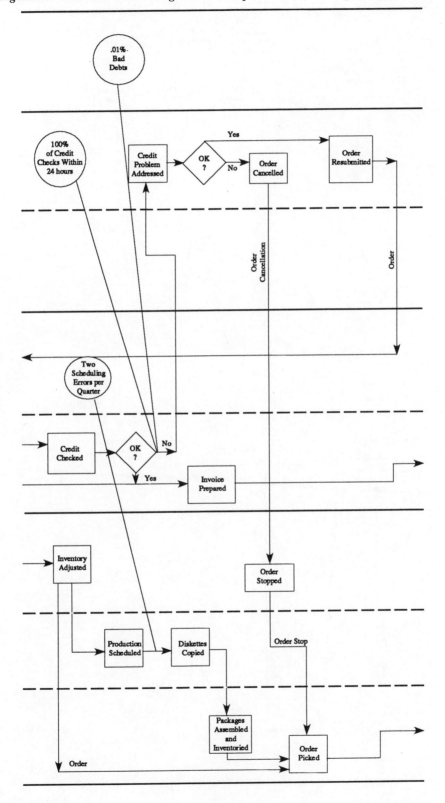

Figure 5.3. Selected Process Subgoals for Computec's Order-Filling Process, Cont'd.

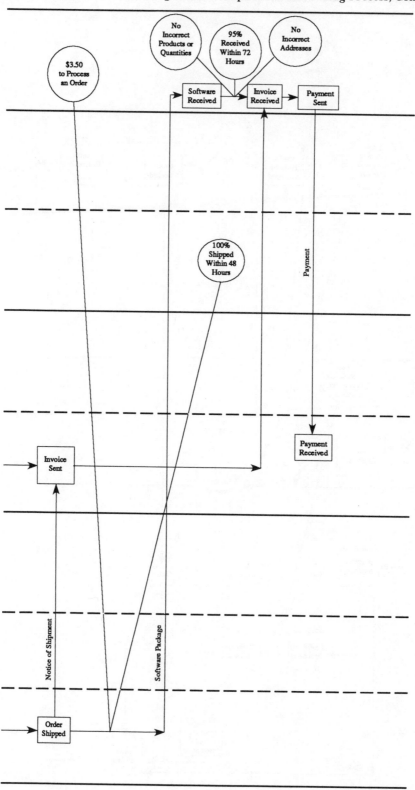

Table 5.2. Selected Functional Goals Based on Computec Order-Filling Process Goals.

Functional Goals Summary (Measures & Goals)

FUNCTION	Timeliness Measures	Goals	Quality Measures	Goals	Budget Measures	Goals	Other Measures	Goals
TOTAL PROCESS	% Orders Received By Customer Within 72 Hours Of Computec Receipt	95	% Orders Correct	100	Avg. Handling Cost / Order	$3.50	% Bad Debts / Inventory Turns	.01 / 60
SALES	% Orders Entered Within 10 Hours Of Receipt	100	% Orders Correct	100				
SALES ADMINISTRATION								
CREDIT & INVOICING	% Credit Checks Done Within 24 Hours Of Order Receipt	100			Processing Cost Per Order	$.50	% Bad Debt	.01
PRODUCTION CONTROL					Processing Cost Per Order	$.50	Inventory Turns	60
COPYING			# of Scheduling Errors /Qtr.	2				
ASSEMBLY & SHIPPING	% Orders Shipped Within 4 Hours of Receipt	100	% Accurate Orders	100	Processing Cost Per Order	$2.50		

presentations are rewarded with the largest budgets and headcount allocations.

Process-driven resource allocation is the result of a determination of the dollars and people required for the process to achieve its goals. After that is done, each function is allocated its share of the resources, according to its contribution to the process. If Process Management is institutionalized throughout an organization, each function's budget is the sum total of its portion of each process budget.

In Computec, for example, resources should be allocated to each step in the order-filling process, according to the quality, timeliness, and cost goals established for that process. Then the various functions should receive the resources they require to make their contributions to that process. For example, the process budget may be divided into order entry, credit checking, scheduling, picking, and shipping. Each of these process segments should receive an appropriate chunk of the process budget. The functions responsible for these process segments should therefore receive budgets sufficient for making their process contributions.

4. *Interface Management*: A Process Map (Figure 5.2) clearly displays the points at which one function (horizontal band on the map) provides a product or service to another function. At each of these points, there is a customer-supplier interface. As we discussed in Chapter Two, these interfaces often represent the greatest opportunity for performance improvement. A process-oriented manager closely monitors interfaces and removes any barriers to effectiveness and efficiency.

As the Computec Process Map shows, the interfaces between Sales and Production Control and between Production Control and Assembly are particularly critical to the success of the order-filling process. Senior management and the Process Owner should pay particular attention to this "white space." To ensure proper attention, they should establish and monitor measures that indicate the quality and efficiency of these interfaces.

The Process Management questions are:

- Have appropriate process subgoals been set?
- Is process performance managed?
- Are sufficient resources allocated to each process?
- Are the interfaces between process steps being managed?

Summary

Work gets done in an organization through its customer and administrative processes. If you want to understand the way work gets done, to improve the way work gets done, and to manage the way work gets done, processes should be the focus of your attention and actions. Viewing business issues from a process perspective often reveals a need to make radical changes in goals, in the design of business systems, and in management practices. The Process Level of Performance has significant implications for:

- *Executives*, who can use the process perspective and tools to link Organization Goals to individual performance, measure what's really going on in the business, benchmark performance against other companies, establish competitive advantages, assess the impact of mergers and acquisitions, and evaluate alternative organization structures
- *Managers*, who can use the process perspective and tools to identify and close quality, cost, and cycle time gaps; manage the interfaces with other departments and the interfaces within their own departments; implement change; and effectively allocate resources
- *Analysts*, who can use the process perspective and tools to diagnose business needs and recommend improvements that will have a significant impact on organization performance, to evaluate actions they are asked to take, and to facilitate improvement teams

If we had to pick one of the Three Levels as the area of greatest opportunity for most organizations, it would be the Process Level. Perhaps that is because it tends to be the least understood and therefore the least managed Level of Performance. Perhaps it is because work gets done through processes. Perhaps it is because it is the middle Level and, as such, serves as the linking pin between the goals, the design, and the management at the Organization Level and at the Job/Performer Level. Or perhaps it is because application of the process tools can address some of the most fundamental needs facing organizations—building a customer-focused organization, quickly and intelligently adapting to new situations, implementing change, and breaking down barriers between departments.

Regardless of the reasons, the Process Level represents a wealth of largely untapped potential. We are learning that it is not enough to manage results. The way in which those results are achieved (the process) is also important. If we *are* achieving the results, we need to know why. If we are *not* achieving the results, we need to know why. In both cases, to a great degree, the answer lies in the process. Once we have processes designed and managed to meet Organization Goals efficiently, we can address the needs of the Job/Performer Level, which is covered in the next chapter.

CHAPTER 6

THE JOB/PERFORMER LEVEL OF PERFORMANCE

What is the city but the people?

— *William Shakespeare*

We could replace Shakespeare's *city* with the word *organization*. Perhaps as a result of its efforts at Levels I and II, Computec, Inc., may have clear Organization and Process Goals. Its organization structure and its process flows may be logical, and its organization and process subgoals, resources, and interfaces may be effectively managed. However, that's not enough. By addressing the needs at the Organization and Process Levels, Computec has established a firm performance foundation. It now needs to construct a building on that foundation. That building is the performance of its people.

In Chapters Four and Five, we focused on systems, not because effective systems compensate for ineffective people but because ineffective systems hinder potentially effective people. Our experience has led us to a bias: most people want to do a good job. However, if you pit a good performer against a bad system, the system will win almost every time.

What Is the Job/Performer Level?

The Job/Performer Level is so named because it looks at jobs and at the people (performers) who serve in those jobs regardless of the level in the organization hierarchy. At this Performance Level, we take the same systems view that we take at the Organization and Process Levels. We believe that performance can be improved only if jobs and performers are analyzed in an overall performance context. The need for a systems perspective is best illustrated by an examination of managers' typical responses to people problems. Aside from the all-too-frequent response of ignoring the problem, the actions we see most often are:

Figure 6.1. The Human Performance System.

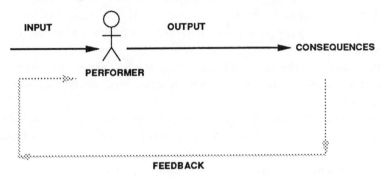

- Train them
- Transfer them
- Coach and counsel them
- Threaten them
- Discipline them
- Replace them

The common theme through all of these responses is *them*. Each action assumes that "them" is what's broken, and therefore "them" is what needs to be fixed.

Assuming that defective people are at the root of all performance problems is as illogical as assuming that a bad battery is at the root of all automobile malfunctions. While the battery may be at fault, a good mechanic realizes that it is part of an engine system. A number of components of that system may harbor the cause of the problem. Even if the battery is performing inadequately, it may be because of another component; the root cause may lie elsewhere in the engine. Similarly, we believe that people are one part of a "performance engine"—the Human Performance System—which has a number of components that influence performance.

The goals, design, and management at the Organization and Process Levels are part of the system that affects human performance. The Human Performance System builds on those Levels by providing a more "micro" picture of people and of the immediate environment that surrounds them. The Human Performance System is displayed in Figure 6.1. As Figure 6.1 shows, our view of the Job/Performer Level reflects the input-process-output-feedback perspective that also underpins the Organization and Process Levels.

Inputs are those raw materials, forms, assignments, and customer requests that cause people to perform. The input package also includes the performers' resources and the systems and procedures that represent the performers' link to the Process Level. For salespeople, the inputs may include leads, territory assignments, and market research information. Their resource inputs may include brochures, presentation aids, and product specifications. Lastly, the salespeople are expected to follow the steps in the sales process.

Performers are the individuals or groups who convert inputs to outputs. Salespeople, sales managers, market researchers, and customers are all performers.

Outputs are the products produced by the performers as their contribution to Organization and Process Goals. People's traits, skills and knowledge, and behaviors are all important performance variables. However, they are all means to the end that justifies the performers' existence in the organization — the outputs. The key output of salespeople is the sales volume they produce.

Consequences are the positive and negative effects that performers experience when they produce an output. Positive consequences may include bonuses, recognition, and more challenging work. Negative consequences include complaints, disciplinary action, and less interesting work. A consequence is determined to be positive or negative according to the unique perspective of each performer. The salespeople who bring in a lot of business may receive healthy commissions and public recognition, which they probably perceive to be positive consequences. Salespeople who fail to meet their quotas may receive the negative consequences of dismissal or reassignment to undesirable, back-office jobs.

Feedback is information that tells performers what and how well they are doing. Feedback can come from error reports, statistical compilations, rejects, oral or written comments, surveys, and performance appraisals. Salespeople get feedback from customers (who buy or don't buy), from sales managers (who may compile sales-performance information), and from the people who produce or deliver the product or service (who may comment on the quality of the sale).

The quality of outputs is a function of the quality of inputs, performers, consequences, and feedback. At the Job/Performer Level, we systematically analyze and improve each of the five Human Performance System components. We believe that comprehensive performance improvement results only from addressing each of the components.

Taking Action at the Job/Performer Level

In Chapters Three, Four, and Five, we discussed the consequences of taking action at the Job/Performer Level without addressing the Performance Variables at the Organization and Process Levels. The risk of failing to address the Job/Performer Level is just as serious: organization and process improvements will not take root if they are not built into jobs. *If jobs are not designed to support process steps, and if job environments are not structured to enable*

Figure 6.2. Hierarchy of Performance Goal Setting.

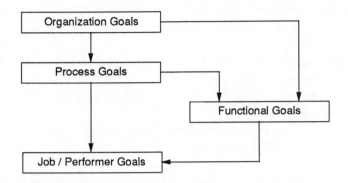

people to make their maximum contributions to process effectiveness and efficiency, then Organization and Process Goals will not be met.

For example, managers in an electronics manufacturing company identified order-to-delivery cycle time as a major competitive disadvantage (Organization Level). To address this disadvantage, they designed a far superior forecasting system for sales and production (Process Level). So far, so good. However, in their enthusiasm for the new process and its potential benefits, they announced and launched it as soon as the ink was dry. They did not identify the changes that were needed in the jobs affected by the new process, nor did they identify the resources and management practices required to support the new process. As a result, the launch of the new system was lengthy, painful, and more costly than necessary.

These managers failed to realize that *the Job/Performer Level does not automatically fall in line with changes at the Organization and Process Levels.* The only way to ensure that people make their maximum possible contributions to Organization and Process Goals is to address each of the three Job/Performer Performance Variables—Job/Performer Goals, Job Design, and Job/Performer Management.

The Performance Variables at the Job/Performer Level

Job/Performer Goals. Since the role of people is to make processes work, we need to make sure that their goals reflect process contributions. Figure 6.2 shows the links between Job/Performer Goals and goals at the other levels.

The major distinction between this goal "flow-down" and traditional approaches is the process (rather than functional) orientation. While Job/Performer Goals should be directly linked to functional goals, both should be derived from the processes they support. To continue our software company example, Computec identified order filling as a strategically significant cross-functional process. A critical step in that process involves checking the credit of a new customer. A process goal (shared by the Finance Department) is to accurately perform a credit check within twenty-four hours of receipt of the order. That goal translates into a set of goals for Finance Clerks:

- 100 percent of credit checks should be conducted within twenty-four hours of order receipt.
- 100 percent of bad credit reports should be returned to a Sales Representative for resolution.
- No more than 1 percent of customers supposedly approvable should turn out to have insufficient credit.

These goals communicate to performers *what* they are expected to do and *how well* they are expected to do it. These two ingredients specify the output component of the Human Performance System. For many performers, the "how well" (performance standard) dimension is missing. Without standards, performers cannot fully understand the level of performance they are expected to attain. We have found that the best way to build understanding of and commitment to Job/Performer Goals is to involve people in the process of establishing the goals for their jobs.

The purpose of Job/Performer goal setting is to arrive at an affirmative answer to this question:

- Are job outputs and standards linked to process requirements, which are in turn linked to customer and organization requirements?

Job Design. Having established the Job/Performer Goals, we need to ensure that each job is structured to enable its incumbents to achieve these goals. Job Design is a function of:

- Allocation of responsibilities among jobs
- Sequence of job activities
- Job policies and procedures
- Ergonomics

When we establish Job Goals based on process requirements, we frequently find that jobs are cluttered with responsibilities that hamper incumbents' ability to support processes. For example, we studied the Buyer position in an oil company. We found that the Buyers' contribution to the purchasing process was diminished by administrative tasks, which took up a significant amount of their time. These responsibilities were transferred to a newly created position, Assistant Buyer. This reallocation of responsibilities freed the Buyers to do what they do best—buy. In addition to establishing a new career path, the creation of this job enabled the process to function more efficiently, without compromising quality.

To help describe Job Goals and to ensure that responsibilities are allocated to appropriate jobs, we recommend constructing a Role/Responsibility Matrix. An example (using Computec) appears in Table 6.1.

The second dimension of Job Design is the sequence of job activities—the *process*—that performers go through to produce their outputs. For example, if Buyers are expected to justify the expenditure of a certain amount of money *before* they can talk to potential vendors and obtain competitive bids, they may not be able to make their maximum contribution to the purchasing process.

Because they are closely linked to the sequence of job activities, job policies and procedures can significantly help or hinder process effectiveness. For example, if the sole-source policy and the Capital Expenditure Request Form are convoluted, Buyers' performance will not reach its potential.

Lastly, the job's ergonomics must support optimum performance. The design of the work station and the physical environment should present few if any barriers to meeting Job/Performer Goals. The Buyers, for example, spend quite a bit of time working with their computers. Chair and table height, screen angle, and lighting should be designed for ease of computer use.

To continue our Computec example, we want to make sure that it makes sense for Finance Clerks to do credit checks, that they have a logical process for credit checking, that they have a set of policies and guidelines for credit checking, and that their work stations are conducive to optimum credit-checking performance.

These are the questions for the variable of Job Design:

- Are process requirements reflected in the appropriate jobs?
- Are job steps in a logical sequence?
- Have supportive policies and procedures been developed?
- Is the job environment ergonomically sound?

Job/Performance Management. Managing the Job/Performer Level is managing the five components of the Human Performance System depicted in Figure 6.1. We have found that six factors affect the effectiveness and efficiency of the Human Performance System. These factors are depicted in Figure 6.3.

The purpose of Job/Performer Management is to put capable people in an environment that supports their accomplishment of Job Goals. Factors 5 and 6 in

Table 6.1. Role/Responsibility Matrix for Finance Function and Customer Order Process.

Major Process Step	Finance Function Accomplishments	FINANCE JOBS, RESPONSIBILITIES, & GOALS					
		CLERK A		CLERK B		CREDIT SUPERVISOR	
		Accomplishments	Goals	Accomplishments	Goals	Accomplishments	Goals
2. Order Entered	• Order Received	• Order Checked for Completeness	• Ø Undetected Errors • 90% of Omissions Returned to Sales Within 8 Hours of Receipt				
	• Customer Status Determined	• Customer Status Checked in File	• Ø Errors in Customer Status Info				
	• Credit Checked (New Customer)			• Customer Credit Checked	• .1% "OK's" Have Bad Credit • 100% Checked Within 24 Hours of Receipt		
				• If OK, Order Updated	• 100% of Orders Updated Within 24 Hours of Receipt		
				• If not OK, Sales Rep Informed	• 100% of "Not OK's" Returned to Sales for Resolution		
6. Order Shipped & Invoiced	• Order Invoiced						

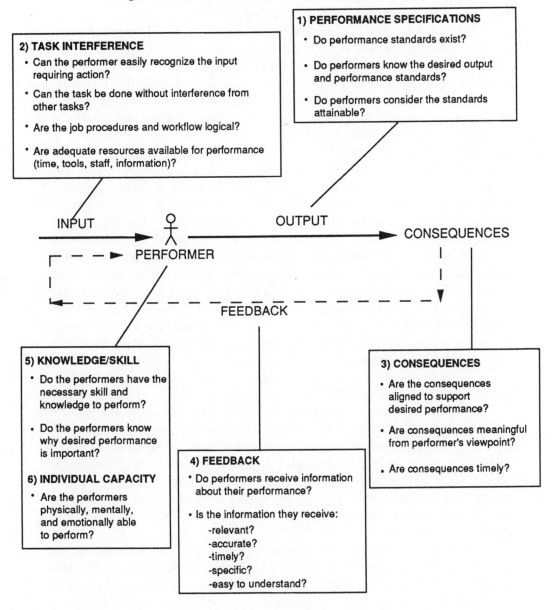

Figure 6.3. Factors Affecting the Human Performance System.

Figure 6.3 address the capability of the performers. Factors 1 through 4 list the factors in a supportive environment.

1. *Performance Specifications* are the outputs and standards that comprise the Job Goals. A manager who participatively establishes process-driven Job/Performer Goals is taking steps to ensure that the questions behind this factor are answered affirmatively. By contrast, the answers are *no*

for salespeople who are not clear on the mix of products they are expected to sell. They have a Performance Specification deficiency.

2. *Task Interference* is partially addressed by Job Design. A well-structured job (in a well-structured process) contains easily recognized high-quality inputs, minimal interference, and logical procedures. Managers who want to minimize Task Interference take one additional step. They provide their people with adequate resources to do the job. For example, the volume of paperwork may take a significant amount of salespeople's time away from their primary responsibility — selling. If so, their selling performance is impeded by Task Interference.

3. *Consequences* must support efficient achievement of Job Goals. Because of a strategic (Organization Level) thrust, one of a salesperson's Job Goals may be to sell a certain volume of new products. If the commission system supports selling the old products, the salesperson's consequences are not aligned to support desired performance. The consequences must also be meaningful to the performer. A given salesperson may not perceive a promotion to sales manager as a positive consequence. Lastly, consequences must occur quickly enough to provide an ongoing incentive. A salesperson who does want to be a sales manager is unlikely to find that consequence sufficiently motivating if he or she cannot reasonably expect it to be delivered in the next five years. The promotion is aligned to support desired performance but does not come quickly enough to serve as the sole incentive.

4. *Feedback* tells a performer to change performance or to keep on performing the same way. *Without feedback, good performance can fall off track, and poor performance can remain unimproved.* Effective feedback meets the criteria listed in Figure 6.3. If feedback is delivered only to the sales force as a whole, individual salespeople may not perceive it as relevant or be able to use it to guide their performance. If feedback is provided only during an annual performance review, it is probably not timely enough to be effective. If feedback is not specific ("Good job" or "Please strengthen that forecast next time"), it will fail to make its contribution to the effectiveness of the Human Performance System.

5. *Skills and Knowledge* are required in any job. If they are missing, job performance is impaired and training may be required. Included in this category is not only the official way of doing the job but also hints and shortcuts ("tribal knowledge") that enable some performers to be exemplary. Salespeople need to know their product/service lines and be skilled in the techniques of selling.

6. *Individual Capacity* involves performers' internal capabilities. No matter how supportive their environment (Factors 1–4) or effective their training (Factor 5), they will not be able to do their jobs if they lack the physical, mental, or emotional capacity to achieve the goals. A salesperson who cannot take rejection may have an Individual Capacity deficiency.

People occasionally tell us that we've missed a factor. They indicate that the key performance variable is motivation (or desire, or drive, or attitude, or morale). We agree. However, motivation is a symptom. When we look behind weak (or strong) motivation, we find our six factors. *If capable (Factor 6), well-trained (Factor 5) people are placed in a setting with clear expectations (Factor 1), minimal task interference (Factor 2), reinforcing consequences (Factor 3), and appropriate feedback (Factor 4), then they will be motivated.*

As the examples illustrate, one powerful use of the questions in Figure 6.3 is as a troubleshooting checklist. Each *no* answer represents some "dirt in the performance engine" and an opportunity for performance improvement. In our experience, the highest percentage of performance opportunities can be found in the environment (Factors 1–4) in which performers work. While the figure varies somewhat in different jobs, industries, and countries, *we have found that about 80 percent of performance improvement opportunities reside in the environment*. Usually, 15 to 20 percent of the opportunities are in the Skills and Knowledge area. We have found that fewer than 1 percent of performance problems result from Individual Capacity deficiencies.

Our experience is consistent with that of Deming (1982), who maintains that only 15 percent of performance problems are worker problems and 85 percent are management problems. Since the odds are against the performer being the broken component of the Human Performance System, the typical management responses to performance problems (listed at the beginning of this chapter) are not likely to address the need.

We have presented the Human Performance System and its related questions as a diagnostic tool. The bad news is that diagnosing a situation does not in itself bring about performance improvement. The good news is that each diagnosed deficiency within the six factors (each *no* answer) suggests an action.

To address the need for clear *Performance Specifications*, we recommend creating a Job Model, which specifies the outputs and standards that are linked to process requirements. (The Job Model format is presented in Chapter Eleven.)

To remove *Task Interference*, restructure the job so that it has clear inputs, a logical sequence of activities, minimal interference among tasks, and sufficient resources. While job design can be difficult, most large organizations have analysts who have expertise in this area. If these skills are not available, a work team of incumbents, supervisors, and analysts can usually, without any sophisticated technology, make the changes necessary to remove the most significant forms of Task Interference.

Consequence deficiencies can be eliminated by adding positive consequences and removing negative consequences for desired responses. While this may sound like it requires one or two degrees in psychology, it doesn't. Performers are very willing to tell anyone who will listen what they find punishing and what incentives work for them. Again, an organization that does not have resident expertise in this area can draw on the collective wisdom of a team of incumbents and supervisors and, perhaps, an analyst.

Designing an effective *Feedback* system tends to require a bit more specialized background. However, an informal system may be all that is needed. The objective is to develop an efficient means of regularly and frequently providing specific performance information to people. The sole feedback mechanism in many organizations is the annual performance appraisal process. However, most appraisal systems are weak in two key feedback areas: frequency and specificity. A manager or analyst who is not able to change the formal performance appraisal form or process must develop other ways to get people the feedback they need when they need it.

To overcome deficiencies in *Skills and Knowledge*, provide classroom training, on-the-job training, and/or a job aid. While training and job-aid design require a body of expertise, those skills usually reside within an organization's Human Resource Development department.

The action to address an *Individual Capacity* deficiency depends on the nature of the deficiency. One of three responses is appropriate: change the job to fit the person (for example, redesign the work station to accommodate a wheelchair), develop the person to fit the job (for example, arrange for counselling in coping with stress), or remove the person from the job (for example, transfer him or her to a job that doesn't require mathematics).

There are lots of great medications out there. Training, for example, is an effective cure. However, it treats only the disease known as a Skills and Knowledge deficiency. It won't ease the pain of the other five afflictions. Another popular treatment is reorganization. An effective reorganization can remove some types of Task Interference but will do little to address other needs. *The net message is that one should diagnose the need before implementing a solution.*

Diagnosing and overcoming deficiencies represents only one of three uses of the Human Performance System. *The six factors can also be used to improve performance that is already meeting expectations.* Any improvement in Feedback, for example, or in elimination of Task Interference will make good performance even better. *Managers and analysts can also use the questions as a checklist, which can help them create a supportive environment around a **new or changed** job.* For example, they can design clear Performance Specifications and structure reinforcing Consequences before the job is created and filled.

There's yet another benefit. *While each enhancement of the Human Performance System improves the quality and efficiency of performance, it also enriches the quality of work life. As a result, performers are willing partners in all three applications of the tool.*

In Computec, Finance Clerks need:

- To understand their three credit-checking goals
- To have manuals, phones, credit-history information, calculators, and other resources required to check credit

- To be rewarded for reaching or exceeding their Job Goals
- To receive frequent, specific feedback on their credit-checking performance
- To know the what, why, and how of effective and efficient credit checking
- To be mentally and emotionally able to conduct credit checks in the environment of the Finance Department

At a high level, these are the questions for Job/Performer Management:

- Do the performers understand the Job Goals (the outputs they are expected to produce and the standards they are expected to meet)?
- Do the performers have sufficient resources, clear signals and priorities, and a logical job design?
- Are the performers rewarded for achieving the Job Goals?
- Do the performers know if they are meeting the Job Goals?
- Do the performers have the necessary skills and knowledge to achieve the Job Goals?
- If the performers were in an environment in which the five questions listed above were answered *yes*, would they have the physical, mental, and emotional capacity to achieve the Job Goals?

Summary

Organization and Process Goals can be achieved only through performance at the Job/Performer Level. Managing people is not easy, but it's less mystical than it may seem. Rather than hiring good people and hoping for efficient, high-quality performance, effective managers use the Human Performance System to manage the factors that enable those good people to perform at an exemplary level. Managers recognize that everyone is in a Human Performance System and that six factors influence the effectiveness of that system. Furthermore, they realize that the four environmental factors (which are largely within their control) tend to harbor the greatest opportunities for performance improvement. We have found that:

- *Executives* can use the Job/Performer Level's outlook and tools to clarify the responsibilities and measure the performance of their direct reports; to ensure that the Human Performance System will and can support the policies that they are considering issuing; to create Human Performance Systems that maximize the quality of outputs, productivity, and quality of work life of their direct reports; to diagnose and improve *their own* Human Performance Systems; and to ensure that organizationwide changes are supported by the environments in which they will be carried out.

- *Managers* can use the Job/Performer Level's outlook in the same ways as executives for their direct reports, themselves, and the changes they manage.
- *Analysts* (especially human resource specialists, industrial engineers, and systems analysts) can use the Job/Performer Level's outlook and tools to diagnose and address performance needs, to ensure that the changes they recommend or are asked to make are supported by the Human Performance System, to manage their bosses and others with whom they have to work, and to diagnose and improve their own performance and enhance the quality of their own work life.

The concepts and tools in this chapter are used throughout the "application" chapters that follow.

PART THREE:
APPLYING
THE THREE LEVELS
OF PERFORMANCE

.▪▪▪.

CHAPTER 7

LINKING PERFORMANCE TO STRATEGY

The bravest are surely those who have the clearest vision of what is before them, glory and danger alike, and yet notwithstanding go out to meet it.

— Thucydides

Before performance at any level can be managed, the expectations for that performance need to be clearly established and communicated. This need is particularly strong at the organization level. If we have not clearly defined the business we are in, we certainly cannot effectively design and manage the Organization Level of performance or establish goals, structure, and management practices at the Process and Job/Performer Levels. Without the guiding hand of a clear strategy, we cannot be sure that we are allocating our resources appropriately, managing our critical business processes, and rewarding the right job performance. To slightly alter the old Chinese proverb, "If we don't know where we are going, any processes and jobs will get us there."

We will not add to the vast number of models, theories, and methodologies for strategic planning. Our objective is to identify those questions that need to be answered if an organization's strategy is going to effectively guide the Three Levels of Performance. A clear strategy leads to a set of superordinate Organization Goals, which should drive the nine Performance Variables depicted in Table 7.1.

What Is Strategy?

Organization strategy is made up of two parts: strategy development and strategy implementation. At the core of strategy development are four elements:

1. Products and services we will offer (*what* we are going to do).
2. Customers and markets we will serve (*whom* we will do it for).

Table 7.1. Strategy's Position in the Nine Performance Variables.

Performance Levels

	GOALS	DESIGN	MANAGEMENT
ORGANIZATION LEVEL	**ORGANIZATION GOALS** • Has the organization's strategy/direction been articulated and communicated? • Does this strategy make sense, in terms of the external threats and opportunities and the internal strengths and weaknesses? • Given this strategy, have the required outputs of the organization and the level of performance expected from each output been determined and communicated?	**ORGANIZATION DESIGN** • Are all relevant functions in place? • Are there unnecessary functions? • Is the current flow of inputs and outputs between functions appropriate? • Does the formal organization structure support the strategy and enhance the efficiency of the system?	**ORGANIZATION MANAGEMENT** • Have appropriate function goals been set? • Is relevant performance measured? • Are resources appropriately allocated? • Are the interfaces between functions being managed?
PROCESS LEVEL	**PROCESS GOALS** • Are goals for key processes linked to customer/organization requirements?	**PROCESS DESIGN** • Is this the most efficient/effective process for accomplishing the Process Goals?	**PROCESS MANAGEMENT** • Have appropriate process sub-goals been set? • Is process performance managed? • Are sufficient resources allocated to each process? • Are the interfaces between process steps being managed?
JOB / PERFORMER LEVEL	**JOB / PERFORMER GOALS** • Are job outputs and standards linked to process requirements (which are in turn linked to customer and organization requirements?)	**JOB DESIGN** • Are process requirements reflected in the appropriate jobs? • Are job steps in a logical sequence? • Have supportive policies and procedures been developed? • Is the job environment ergonomically sound?	**JOB / PERFORMER MANAGEMENT** • Do the performers understand the Job Goals (outputs they are expected to produce and the standards they are expected to meet)? • Do the performers have sufficient resources, clear signals and priorities, and a logical job design? • Are the performers rewarded for achieving the Job Goals? • Do the performers know if they are meeting the Job Goals? • Do the performers have the necessary knowledge/skill to achieve the Job Goals? • If the performers were in an environment in which the five questions listed above were answered "yes," would they have the physical, mental, and emotional capacity to achieve the Job Goals?

3. Competitive advantages (*why* the customers will buy from us).
4. Product and market priorities (*where* we will place our emphasis).

At the core of strategy implementation is a fifth, multifaceted, element:

5. Systems and structures (*how* we are going to bring about the *what, who, why,* and *where*).

We are not implying that these five elements are all there is to strategy. However, we believe that all other strategic analysis, decisions, and actions are either:

- Inputs to the first four elements (market research, industry analysis, competitive analysis, environmental monitoring, portfolio planning)
- Ways of measuring the effectiveness of the first four elements (financial results, market share, nonfinancial critical success factors)
- Philosophical guides to all five elements (values, culture)
- Subparts of the fifth element (budgets, marketing plans, human resource plans, technology plans)
- Problem solving and action planning to remove barriers to the fifth element

What are the questions that top managers (of an entire organization or of any component within an organization) need to answer before they can design and manage organization performance?

Questions that precede strategic decision making:

1. What values are going to guide our business?
2. How far down the road are we going to look?
3. What assumptions about the external environment (regulation, the economy, resource availability, technology, competition, the market) underpin our strategy?

Questions that address products and services (Element 1):

4. What existing and new products and services will we be offering (and not offering)?
5. What criteria will we use to evaluate a new product or service opportunity?

Questions that address customers and markets (Element 2):

6. What existing and new customer groups will we be serving (and not serving)?
7. What criteria will we use to evaluate a new market opportunity?

Questions that address competitive advantages (Element 3):

8. What factors (price and/or the various dimensions of quality) are meaningful to our customers?
9. Which of these factors will represent our competitive advantages?

Questions that address product and market emphasis (Element 4):

10. In which of our current product or market areas will we be placing the greatest emphasis (resources and attention)?
11. In what new product or market areas will we be placing the greatest emphasis?

Figure 7.1 shows how the answers to these questions help us effectively define each part of the systems view of performance, which we introduced in Chapter Two.

Without answers to questions 1 through 11, the organizational ship has no rudder. Without strategic definition and goals, which position an organization in its environment, performance management is at best a guessing game. We subscribe to the old saw that says an organization needs not only to do things right but also to do the right things. The right things are those activities that are in concert with a viable, comprehensive, and clearly articulated strategy.

Why Do Strategies Fail?

A solid strategy is only half the battle. In our experience, the majority of the strategies that have never come to successful fruition have not failed because they lack a clear, viable vision; they are gathering dust because they have been poorly implemented. Unfortunately, even the best strategies do not spontaneously guide performance. Comprehensive actions to implement a strategy must be planned, carried out, and monitored. Moreover, no matter how talented and hardworking they may be, top managers cannot implement a strategy by themselves. A key implementation contribution must be made by middle managers and by those others who manage the systems and people who will make or break the strategy.

An early implementation step should be widespread communication of the strategy. The downside of communication (a possible leak to competitors of information that they probably know anyway, just by observation

Figure 7.1. The Impact of Strategy on the Components of an Organization System.

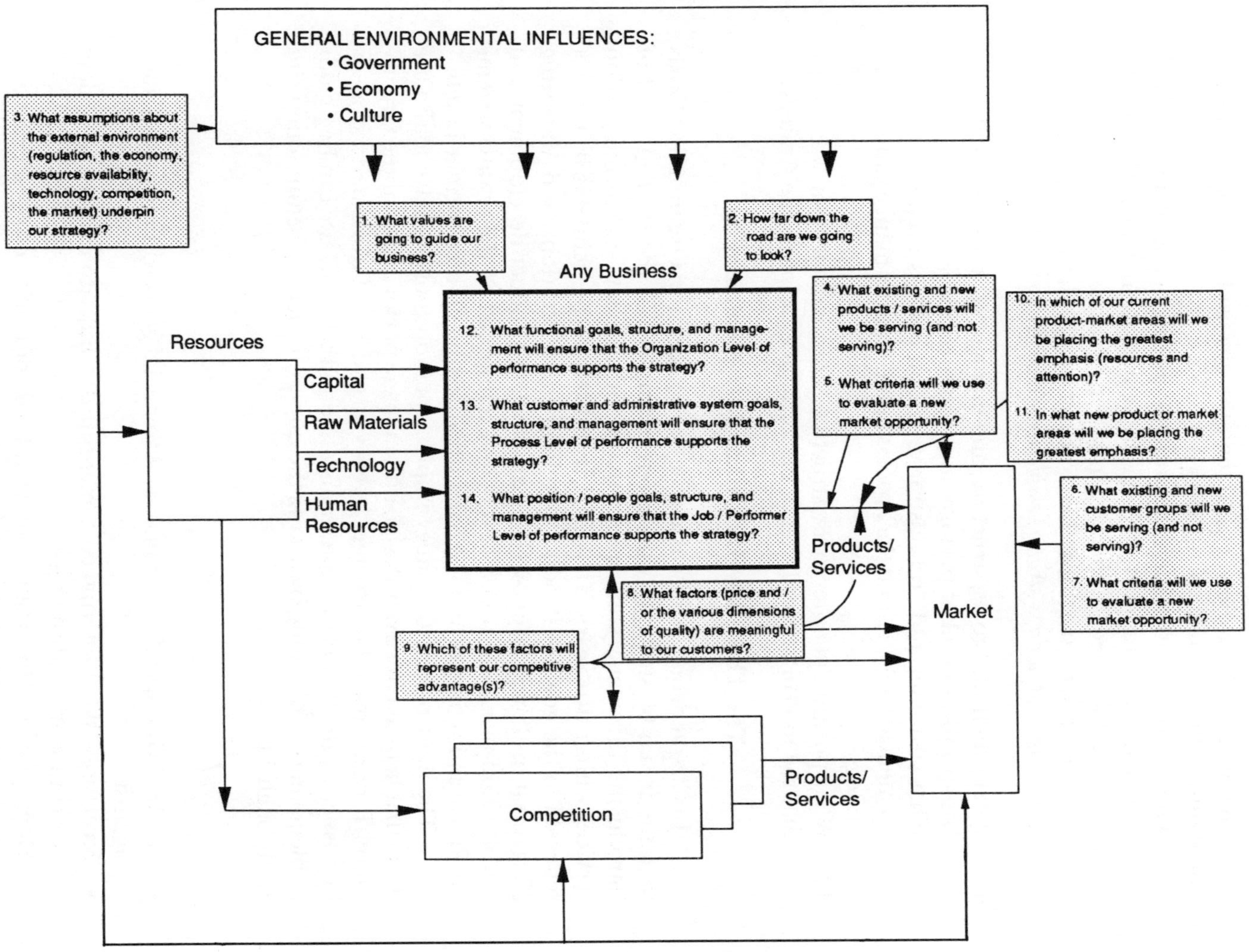

in the marketplace) is far less serious than the downside of noncommunication (failure to implement the strategy).

Once people understand the strategy, management should establish an infrastructure that supports strategy implementation. That infrastructure needs to be established at the Organization, Process, and Job/Performer Levels. To our eleven questions, therefore, let us add three more:

Questions that address strategy implementation (Element 5):

12. What functional goals, structure, and management will ensure that the Organization Level of performance supports the strategy?
13. What customer and administrative system goals, structure, and management will ensure that the Process Level of performance supports the strategy?
14. What position/people goals, structure, and management will ensure that the Job/Performer Level of performance supports the strategy?

The Three Levels of Strategy Implementation

In Chapter Four, we discussed the need to develop Organization Goals that are driven by strategy. Among our examples was the strategic goal of introducing three new software products and two new system integration services within two years. That goal is unlikely to be achieved if it is not reflected in the goals of Product Development, Operations, and Marketing (Organization Level), supported by an efficient product development and introduction process (Process Level), and reinforced by the reward systems for Research Engineers and the Sales organization (Job/Performer Level).

The most powerful strategy implementation tools we have found are those that help us effectively design and manage performance at the Organization, Process, and Job/Performer levels. Once we have formulated a strategy by answering the first eleven questions listed in Figure 7.1, we can begin our implementation planning by asking the questions that lie behind questions 12 through 14:

Level I

- Goals — What specific customer and financial goals will we set and track against?
- Structure — What internal customer-supplier links do we need to achieve our competitive advantage?
- Management — How many and what kinds of resources need to be allocated to the various functions?

Level II

- Goals — What are the goals for the processes that are critical to our competitive advantage?

- Structure—What are we doing to make sure that our strategically critical processes are working efficiently and effectively?
- Management—How are we making sure that our critical processes are being managed on an ongoing basis?

Level III

- Goals—What are the goals for the jobs that are most critical to process (and, in turn, strategic) success?
- Structure—What are we doing to design each of these key jobs so that it best contributes to strategic success?
- Management—What are we doing (feedback, training, incentives) to create an environment that supports each job's strategic contribution?

The responses to these questions represent the core of a strategy implementation plan. Throughout this book, we present tools—organization mapping, process management, human performance management, measurement—designed to help develop these responses.

Linking Performance to Strategy: An Example

Baldwin Drug Stores, Inc. (a fictional company), is a retail pharmacy and sundries chain. To succeed in its highly competitive industry, Baldwin's executives realize that they need to establish a strategy that clearly guides day-to-day performance. They use the eleven questions to be sure that all of the bases are covered. We can summarize the results of top management's strategy formulation decisions:
    1. They establish a list of value statements. Among them are:

- Baldwin will sell only the highest-quality products.
- Baldwin employees will go the extra mile to provide service that meets or exceeds customers' expectations.
- Because employees are the best source of ideas, the business will be run in a participative, open-door style.

    2. They decide that in their highly turbulent industry a three-year strategy is appropriate.
    3. They use market research information and their own understanding of the industry to document a list of assumptions about the environment in which Baldwin will be doing business three years from now. Some of these assumptions are:

- Easing of pharmaceutical industry regulation will increase the quantity of new drugs and dramatically increase the number of generic drugs.

- The economy in Baldwin's geographical territory will continue to grow.
- Inexpensive full- and part-time cashiers and stockpeople will be increasingly difficult to find.
- Discount drug outlets and superstores will continue to represent the most formidable competition.
- Customers will continue to be willing to pay a bit more if they perceive that they are receiving value beyond that provided by the basic product.

4. The executives, after much debate, decide that they will resist the temptation to offer groceries, automotive products, and toys. They also decide not to manufacture any products. They will continue to offer prescription and patent medicines, health care products, cosmetics, camera supplies, and office supplies. In short, they decide that Baldwin can succeed by continuing to be a chain of old-fashioned corner drug stores. They develop a complete list of categories of products they will and will not offer during the next three years.

5. when evaluating a new product line, the executive team will use these criteria:

- Has the potential to meet profitability goals
- Fits with the "corner drug store" image and the current Baldwin product categories
- Is able to meet an enduring need
- Requires no new forms of display or significantly new employee skills

6. They decide that Baldwin will target three primary markets (customer groups): elderly people, disabled people, and young affluent families. While these niches clearly exclude a large percentage of the population, the top team believes that this focus will enable Baldwin to develop a significant competitive advantage and a thriving business.

7. When evaluating a new market opportunity (be it a new geographical area or a new customer type), the primary "go–no go" criteria will concern whether the area or group of customers has a documented need for the current product line, whether the new venture is able to establish Baldwin's competitive advantages, and whether it requires new investment that can be recouped within two years.

8. To ensure that their strategy is customer-focused, the executives use survey and focus-group information to identify the requirements of customers in the elderly, disabled, and affluent-family markets. They decide that these groups are primarily driven by convenience, product availability, and service. While price is a factor (particularly for Medicare patients), the top team believes that the Baldwin customers will pay a bit more for convenience, availability, and service.

9. Baldwin's competitive advantage will be in the three areas just

identified. Baldwin will establish an advantage in convenience through store locations, business hours, and home delivery. Baldwin will ensure that a full line of products for elderly and disabled people and affluent families is always available. In addition to home delivery, Baldwin's services will include knowledgeable photographic and cosmetics personnel, a medication hot line, and the kind of personal attention that comes from strong relationships with the doctors used by Baldwin's customers. The executives firmly believe that these factors will differentiate Baldwin from the low-service, low-price discount stores, grocery stores, and drug warehouses.

10. During the next three years, Baldwin will place a disproportionate marketing and sourcing emphasis on the patent medications that it currently provides to elderly and disabled people.

11. Given the competitive advantages Baldwin plans to establish, its management will emphasize new products (such as supplies for disabled people) that will enable it to be a "one-stop shopping" store for its target markets.

These eleven points represent only a high-level strategy, but they establish a clear sense of direction and reflect an analysis of all the components of the systems view of performance. To make sure that their vision is *implemented*, Baldwin's top managers take three more actions:

12. They establish a set of organizationwide and departmental goals that reflect their strategic thrusts. First, they establish specific goals for service quality for all departments that have contact with customers. Second, they ensure that all departments are structured and linked in a way that enables Baldwin to provide differentiated customer service. Third, they make sure that resources are appropriately allocated. For example, Market Researchers receive the money and staff they need to gather comprehensive information on the three target markets.

13. They make sure that key processes (customer service, market research, and distributor selection) are documented and have goals that support the strategic goals. They make sure that these strategic processes are efficiently accomplishing their goals, and they install a process management infrastructure to monitor and continuously improve these strategic processes.

14. Within each strategic process, they identify a number of jobs that are particularly critical to organization success. In Baldwin's customer service process, all customer contact jobs are critical. For these jobs, goals (derived from process goals) are established and communicated. The jobs are designed to enhance customer service. Most important, the management team creates an environment (through training, feedback, and rewards) that supports outstanding customer service.

Summary

The Three Levels framework makes two contributions to organization strategy. To strategy *formulation*, it offers the systems framework (see Table

7.1), which ensures that an organization's direction is based on an analysis of all the strategic variables. The systems components suggest eleven questions that an effective strategy should answer.

To strategy *implementation*, the Three Levels framework offers the nine Performance Variables, which must be addressed to ensure that the strategic vision becomes organizational reality. A management team that cascades its strategy through the Organization, Process, and Job/Performer Levels dramatically increases the odds of that strategy's taking root. At each level, the strategy is implemented through Goals, Design, and Management.

Chapters Eight through Fourteen delve more deeply into a variety of dimensions of strategy implementation.

,mmmmmmmmmmmmmmmmmmmmmmmmmmmm,

MOVING FROM
ANNUAL PROGRAMS
TO SUSTAINED
PERFORMANCE IMPROVEMENT

Beware, lest you lose the substance by grasping at the shadow.
—Aesop

At most large and medium-sized organizations, top managers like to embark on performance improvement programs. These programs tend to have a focal slogan, which includes terms like *quality, customer service*, and *teamwork*. They tend to be launched with a great deal of publicity. They are initially supported by a large expenditure of resources (often cited as a symbol of significant support from top management).

Unfortunately, betterment programs frequently end up grasping at the shadow, rather than establishing an infrastructure for substantive, sustained performance improvement. To wit, here is an excerpt from an issue of a *Fortune* 100 company newsletter:

> With the presentations recently of two quality circles, the circle program closed its ledger and ended. From the five pilot circles, the program grew to 327 circles. 93 presentations included cost savings. During its existence, the program became an integral part of the philosophy of participative management. It provided both tangible and intangible results, such as developing problem-solving, leadership, and communication skills.

When it initially became clear that U.S. involvement in the Vietnam war was a no-win proposition, Vermont's Senator Aiken proposed that America declare victory and withdraw. Similarly, this company counted up the number of teams and recommendations, declared the quality circle program a success, and shut it down.

A human resource development professional in this organization (displaying rare commodities — memory and perspective) developed a family tree which positions the quality circle program as one of 36 productivity, quality, participative management, and culture change programs his company has embarked upon in the last ten years. Each of them began with impressive fanfare, lofty expectations, and large budgets. Most are now dead or comatose. It is no surprise that, in this organization, the prevailing employee reaction to any new management initiative is what Chris Hart of the Harvard Business School calls BOHICA—Bend Over, Here It Comes Again. After ten years of programs, employees perceive the organization, with only a few pockets of exception, as the same old place (from a lecture during the GTE Quality: The Competitive Edge program, Norwalk, Conn., July 20, 1987).

The short-term financial perspective of U.S. business has been thoroughly documented and castigated (with little effect) in a number of books and articles during the last few years. This shortness of attention span extends to organization improvement as well. Perhaps American management's impatient search for the magic bullet is at the root of its impressive record in entrepreneurship and product innovation. However, when it comes to substantive, sustained gains in performance, there is no magic bullet.

In our experience, even the most effective training programs and organization development interventions tend to offer only one or two of the many pieces of the performance puzzle. We have found that any improvement effort—whether it is driven by quality, customer focus, productivity, cycle time, cost reduction, or even culture change—is effective only to the degree that it encompasses the Three Levels of Performance.

Four Examples of Flawed Performance Improvement Efforts

How would you grade these performance improvement programs?

Example 1. The president of ABC Electronics, Inc., has been exposed to the "quality" religion and becomes a true believer. Realizing that quality is getting insufficient attention in his company, he:

- Arranges for a "fire and brimstone" quality speaker to deliver a one- or two-day session for all managers
- Directs the Human Resource Development Department to prepare each supervisor to conduct video-plus-discussion sessions with his or her subordinates
- Appoints a full-time Quality Director, who will report directly to him
- Asks the Quality Director to produce a one-paragraph quality statement and circulate it to all employees
- Directs the Employee Communications Department to manage a poster contest, with an award going to the winning design

- Tells the Personnel Department to arrange for all employees to wear badge inserts that say, "Quality—It's as Basic as ABC"
- Provides additional funds to the Human Resource Development Department for the purchase or development of workshops in "Japanese quality techniques"

Example 2. The corporate Quality Director of the Sleep Inns hotel chain hires, at great expense, a top-notch consulting firm to study and recommend improvements in the guest checkin and checkout systems. The consultants involve representatives of supervisory and nonsupervisory front-desk staff in the analysis and development of proposed changes. The recommended improvements are blessed, with only minor modifications, by the Quality Director and by the Vice President for Guest Services. The improvements are implemented, along with a system for measurement and reward, which reinforces accurate and speedy checkin and checkout performance.

Example 3. After extensive market research and competitive assessment, the top management team at the Cars R Us automotive parts company decides that it is going to build a competitive advantage by shortening order processing cycle time—the time that elapses between the customer's placement of an order and the customer's receipt of the correct part. A group of analysts is assigned to examine and recommend ways of reducing the time it takes to execute each of the three processes that affect order processing cycle time and order entry, manufacturing and assembly, and distribution. In three weeks, the analysts have developed systems that, without sacrificing quality or increasing cost, can shorten the cycle time from the current twenty-eight days to eleven days, the best time in the industry. The systems are implemented as recommended.

Example 4. As part of its planning for an increasingly deregulated (competitive) environment, the Universal Telephone Company establishes a strategic objective: to improve, by 10 percent, the ratings on the repair questions that are part of the quarterly customer satisfaction surveys. The policy committee clearly communicates this strategic goal and increases the Repair Department's headcount ceiling and budget allocation for trucks and tools. The Human Resource Development Department is told to extend and enhance repairperson's and repair supervisors' training programs. In each section within the Repair Department, quality teams are formed. Under the guidance of a skilled facilitator, the teams meet once a week to solve problems in their areas.

Analysis

In *Example 1*, the ABC Electronics president has embraced much of the form and little of the substance of an effective quality effort. While his actions are nobly motivated and not necessarily dangerous, he gets an overall grade of F for doing nothing of lasting significance at the Organization, Process, or Job/Performer Level.

There is no evidence that he has articulated a quality strategy for the *organization* or designed the functional relationships through which he will carry it out. He hasn't initiated any efforts to build quality into any strategically critical business *processes*, and the company doesn't appear to have built quality into the measurement, training, feedback, and reward systems of individual *jobs*. This scenario has all the trappings of a short-lived, minimum-impact program.

In *Example 2*, Sleep Inns has done a bit better. It has taken action to improve the performance of a business process (checkin and checkout). The people closest to the action have been involved in the analysis. The Quality Director gets high marks for seeing that the results of the process improvement effort are built into the support systems at the Job/Performer Level. What's missing is the Organization Level. Is checkin/checkout the most strategically significant process? Where is speedy checkout in the customers' priorities? Is the chain attempting to match the competition or establish a competitive edge? Having selected that process, why limit the involvement in the project to the front-desk function? (Doesn't the checkin/checkout process involve the reservations, bell, and accounting staffs as well?) And where is top management? With all due respect to the Quality Director, what signal does top management's absence in this project send to the organization?

Cars R Us, described in *Example 3*, has addressed the strategic dimension of the Organization Level. Order processing cycle time has been designated as a potential competitive advantage. Our question at the Organization Level is this: Have the functions been aligned (in terms of customer-supplier relationships) to achieve the strategic goal? A critical process has been selected and studied. Unfortunately, we can't give this company more than a C at the Process Level because the process analysis was carried out by analysts, rather than by key players in the order process. Involving them would have strengthened their cross-functional relationships and increased their commitment to the changes.

The major shortcoming, however, is at the Job/Performer Level. Here, we have a sin of omission. A clear strategy and a well-structured process are worthless if they do not drive the performance of people. Nothing appears to have been done to incorporate the cycle-time strategy and process improvements into the jobs of people who work in the order processing system.

In *Example 4*, Universal Telephone has established an Organization Level objective to improve performance. The objective is strategic because it addresses customer and competitive concerns. Furthermore, the company has ensured that organizationwide communication and sufficient resource allocation support the objective. The only fly in the Organization Level ointment is the top team's apparent failure to see repair as an area that most likely involves more than just the Repair Department. Training and team problem solving are ensuring that the Job/Performer Level is adequately addressed. (Perhaps it is being addressed *too* adequately; there's no evidence of a Skills/Knowledge deficiency that warrants the investment in training.) The policy committee wisely realizes that the men and women closest to repair are best equipped to develop the most effective improvements. However, the repair process undoubtedly involves handoffs (interfaces) among functions inside and outside Repair. As a result, the functional (section-by-section) approach to the quality team's structure is a bit troublesome. We also wonder whether the improvements that come out of the teams will be adequately supported by the measurement and reward systems.

The major flaw in Universal Telephone's approach is the absence of the link that we most frequently find missing—the Process Level. There is no indication that the repair process is being systematically and holistically addressed. The potential shortcomings in measurement and the likely survival of "white space" issues (see Chapter Two) considerably lower the odds of success in this effort. The Organization Level goal is unlikely to be achieved without the creation of an effective repair process. The team recommendations at the Job/Performer Level are liable to be constrained by any weaknesses in the repair process as a whole, which is beyond the charter of any one sectional team.

Organizationwide Performance Improvement

Our critique of the four attempted performance improvement programs underscores our belief that any effort that does not address all Three Levels of Performance is liable to produce only piecemeal results. If the president of ABC Electronics were to follow the Three Levels approach, he would take nine steps, which mirror the nine Performance Variables discussed in Chapters Three through Six:

Organization Level:

1. Goals—Develop a set of companywide customer-driven performance improvement goals linked to the competitive advantages and/or gaps outlined in the company strategy.
2. Design—Design an organization in which functional customer-supplier relationships support the strategy.
3. Management—Allocate resources so that the goals can be achieved and establish a system for tracking and improving performance.

Process Level:

4. Goals—Identify the processes that are most critical to the strategy and establish goals that describe the performance required of those processes.

5. Design — Charter cross-functional teams to find the disconnects in the current processes and to design processes to eliminate the disconnects.
6. Management — Establish goals at critical junctures in the process and continuously monitor and improve process performance.

Job/Performer Level:

7. Goals — Identify the jobs that are critical to the success of the process and establish goals for the outputs of those jobs.
8. Design — Design and organize the jobs so that they can efficiently and effectively achieve the goals.
9. Management — Create a job environment in which capable, adequately trained people have clear statements of, regular feedback on, positive consequences for, and few barriers to goal achievement.

The president might still want to provide awareness training, appoint a Quality Director, and blanket the organization with posters and badge inserts. However, by addressing the Nine Variables outlined in the Three Levels approach, he would be moving from program-of-the-month symbols to an infrastructure for substantive, long-term performance improvement.

As flawed as it is, the ABC quality program has one major strength — the involvement of the president. We have found few examples of successful and sustained efforts in which senior management is not actively involved. In exemplary programs, top managers do more than give their blessing and some money. Figure 8.1 describes the five responsibilities assumed by top managers who are actively involved in a performance improvement effort.

Two Case Studies

Douglas Aircraft Company. We had the opportunity to help the Douglas Aircraft Company (a division of McDonnell Douglas Corporation) design and implement a companywide performance improvement effort. The top management team was determined to fight the "just another program" (BOHICA) attitude and to implement a quality and productivity effort with teeth.

They began by identifying what they called the company's Significant Business Issue: "Satisfy Your Customer Through First-Time Quality." They set up a structure in which natural work groups, which are either vertical (work-unit groups) or horizontal (cross-functional groups), meet regularly, assisted by line people who are trained as full-time facilitators. The teams go through a five-phase process:

1. The leader presents to the team the competitive reasons for the Significant Business Issue effort and describes the purpose and mechanics of the process.

Figure 8.1. Top Management's Role in a Performance Improvement Effort.

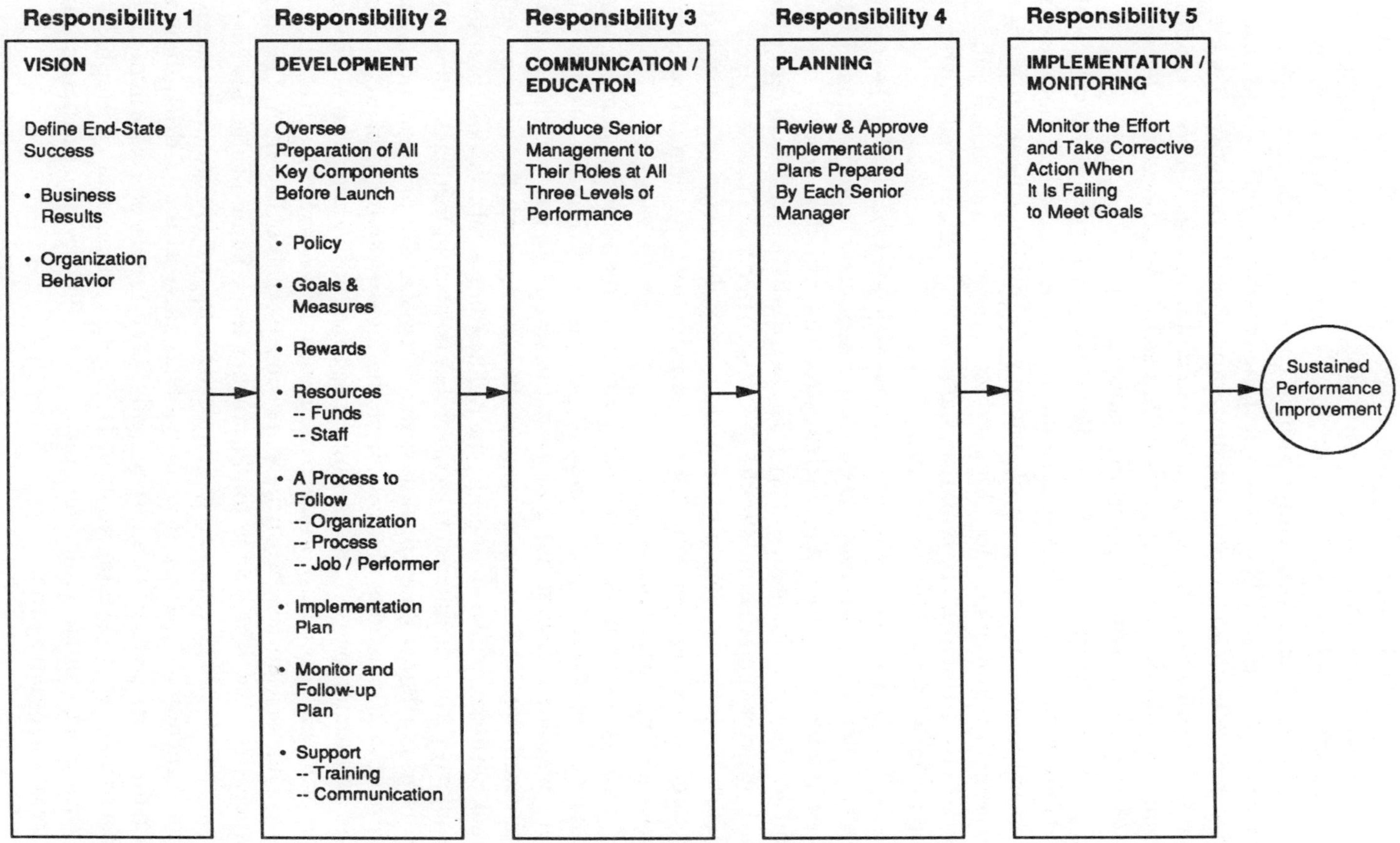

Responsibility 1	Responsibility 2	Responsibility 3	Responsibility 4	Responsibility 5
VISION	**DEVELOPMENT**	**COMMUNICATION / EDUCATION**	**PLANNING**	**IMPLEMENTATION / MONITORING**
Define End-State Success	Oversee Preparation of All Key Components Before Launch	Introduce Senior Management to Their Roles at All Three Levels of Performance	Review & Approve Implementation Plans Prepared By Each Senior Manager	Monitor the Effort and Take Corrective Action When It Is Failing to Meet Goals
• Business Results	• Policy			
• Organization Behavior	• Goals & Measures			
	• Rewards			
	• Resources -- Funds -- Staff			
	• A Process to Follow -- Organization -- Process -- Job / Performer			
	• Implementation Plan			
	• Monitor and Follow-up Plan			
	• Support -- Training -- Communication			

Sustained Performance Improvement

2. On the basis of objectives that have originated with the organization strategy and have flowed down to them through the Program Offices (representing each product line), the team members use a Relationship Map (see Chapter Four) to document their customers, products and services, inputs, and suppliers. They then select the product or service and customer that they believe can have the greatest impact on the objectives. Focused on the key product and customer, they set a tentative goal, which describes the team's contribution to the objective. (Phases 1 and 2 address the *Organization Level* of both the company and the team.)

3. The team selects one or more representatives to interview individuals from the customer organization (which, more often than not, is an internal unit). Through a set of structured questions, the team learns the customer's requirements for the product or service and gets feedback on current performance. The tentative goal from Phase 2 is refined and finalized on the basis of these requirements.

4. The team members use a Process Map (see Chapter Five) to design a process that will enable them to satisfy the customer's requirements with first-time quality (which includes efficiency and cost as well as traditional quality considerations). The team documents any gaps between the current process and this customer-driven "should" process. After the Process Map is completed, the team develops a proposed numerical measure and standard for each customer requirement. These standards are then negotiated with the customer in a second meeting.

5. In the final phase, the team members plan and implement actions to move from the "is" to the "should" process, resolving any problems they have identified during the first four phases. They convert the customer-approved standards into a measurement system, which the unit can use to track performance on an ongoing basis. They then establish a mechanism for regularly gathering data on the customer's needs and feedback. (Phases 3, 4, and this portion of Phase 5 address the *Process Level* of performance.) Lastly, they commit to actions that will drive the measures, the improved process, and a customer-focused mindset into the jobs of individuals who work within the process. (This part of Phase 5 addresses the *Job/Performer Level*.)

It's not a flawless effort; there are some pockets of BOHICA. The formal process is a bit light on the Job/Performer level. Some of the flowed-down objectives do not give specific guidance to the teams. Too few of the teams are cross-functional. However, it is probably as successful as a thirty-thousand-person effort can be. It addresses all Three Levels of Performance. It is sustainable. It is customer-driven. It places a great deal of emphasis on measurement, and it is implemented by individuals within the natural structure of the organization.

GTE. The GTE approach to performance improvement is also based on the Three Levels of Performance, but it is quite different from the one taken by Douglas Aircraft. Rather than establishing teams, the GTE effort uses management team training as the catalyst for performance improvement.

The current thrust began with the corporate Policy Committee's identification of quality as the primary competitive issue in all of GTE's telecommunications, lighting, and precision materials businesses. The Committee members (the top seven executives in the company) returned from their annual strategic-planning retreat with a mandate for executive-level quality training. While the company had taken and was continuing to take a variety of formal steps to enhance quality, most of the programs did not have heavy top-management involvement. The Committee saw this involvement as critical to the success of any quality effort.

Independently, the Vice President for Quality Services, and the Director of Executive Education had also concluded that the next step in the quality journey was senior management's education. They had been working on a quality training and education program, and the Policy Committee's mandate was all they needed to launch their program. The Vice President and the Director broke the mold by developing a training program that met these criteria:

- It is a hands-on workshop, rather than a quality-awareness program.
- It is driven by the need for quality to be a strategic weapon, rather than merely a set of unrelated quality tools.
- It is attended by teams from each business unit. The teams are made up of the business-unit President or General Manager and his or her direct reports.
- The work sessions continue after the formal classroom training. The teams submit their action plans to a Policy Committee member, who holds them accountable for taking the actions and achieving the promised results.

The first group of participants in the workshop, called "Quality: The Competitive Edge" (QCE), was the Policy Committee itself. The members recognized that they needed to learn about quality and commit to specific actions that would enable them to lead the quality effort. Following this session, the President of each of GTE's thirty-five business units, along with his Vice Presidents, attended one of twelve QCE sessions.

According to the primary architect of QCE, "The course itself, and the action plans of the SBU [strategic business unit] teams, was built on a structure we call "The Three Levels of Quality":

Level 1: The Organization Level: Development of a customer-driven quality strategy which supports the SBU business plan

Level 2: The Process Level: The cross-functional work flows which produce outputs for internal and external customers

Level 3: Individuals and Teams: Creating an environment which supports the natural desire of employees to do quality work" (Murphy, 1988).

In the three-day sessions, the teams learned about quality at each of the three levels and spent a significant amount of time in team planning sessions. During these workshop activities, the teams committed to a series of actions at each of the Three Levels of quality.

The 550 executives who attended QCE developed quality strategies for their business units or staff departments, selected tools for implementing those strategies, and planned to engage in specific leadership behaviors to support that implementation. Not surprisingly, the majority of their implementation plans included workshops for the next two or three levels of management. QCE-II was developed to meet this need.

The two-day QCE-II workshop is being offered at the business-unit locations to managers (and occasionally to nonmanagers). QCE-II is a vehicle for these employees to understand the quality strategy developed by their top management and to commit to making the most direct possible contribution to that strategy through the implementation of their own action plans at each of the Three Levels of quality. These action plans are based on the business-unit executives' list of "killer gaps" that currently or potentially represent competitive quality disadvantages. To ensure that QCE-II is not "just another program," the instructors are the business-unit Presidents and Vice Presidents, assisted by videotapes of the QCE-I faculty presentations.

One of the most powerful dimensions of QCE-I and QCE-II involves what we have been calling the Process Level of Performance: "Process Management was recognized by approximately 75% of all teams as the real point of leverage; most were able to identify which processes and which other teams needed to be included in their plans. Their pressure on top management as they collaborate across functions in order to fix broken processes is forcing management to *assume a coordinating role* as opposed to its traditional preference for managing subordinates one on one" (Murphy, 1988; emphasis in original). To respond in more depth to this priority need, a process management workshop has been developed as the third workshop in what has become GTE's quality curriculum.

Assessing the results of QCE-II, Murphy (1988) says: "The impact on employees of this unprecedented commitment is profound. It is immediately apparent to every team attending QCE-II that this is mold-breaking, culture-crashing behavior by their executives. They begin to believe, for the first time, that *this is different*. That this is not going to go away. Their executive leaders are going the last mile to demonstrate their commitment and seriousness, their modeling of risk-taking behavior and their openness as instructors to ideas, feedback, constructive criticism" (emphasis in original).

The GTE QCE effort is a rare example of a training-driven program achieving significant hard (quantitative quality improvement) and soft (culture change) results. Certainly, the commitment from the top of the house, as well as the unflagging efforts of the Vice President for Quality Services and the Director of Executive Education, are key factors in its success. However, a significant amount of the credit also goes to the comprehensive tools and actions taken at each of the Three Levels of Performance.

Summary

Beware of programs. By definition, programs end. Performance improvement, by contrast, should never end. Successful performance improvement efforts tend to meet four criteria:

- They establish an infrastructure, which enables them to be sustained without "special program" mechanisms.
- They are goal-driven. They begin with a set of goals and include a mechanism for reestablishing goals over time.
- They involve substantive actions at the Organization, Process, and Job/ Performer Levels.
- They are driven by the active involvement of the top management in the organization.

The nine Performance Variables provide a checklist of substantive actions that can be taken at each of the Three Levels. However, this performance improvement technology is just the start. An organization's top managers must take responsibility for sticking with the effort and carving out a significant role for themselves.

CHAPTER 9

^^

DIAGNOSING
AND IMPROVING
THE ORGANIZATION:
A CASE STUDY

Medicine, to produce health, has to examine disease.

—Plutarch

The pharmaceutical industry has developed a host of effective medicines. Penicillin, for example, is a drug of demonstrated effectiveness. However, it probably won't help a cataract. There's no evidence that cortisone will do anything for a fever. Aspirin has been called a wonder drug, but it is actually harmful to someone suffering from an ulcer. Unfortunately, every effective medicine addresses only a limited number of ailments. Professional diagnosticians, called doctors, are paid to match medications with patients' illnesses.

Similarly, there are lots of proved performance improvement "medicines" out there. Training is one form of medication. Reorganization is another. A management information system is another. An incentive compensation plan is yet another. The question is, who are the "doctors" being paid to match these (and other) medications with our organizations' illnesses?

Typically, the professionals who are paid to solve organization performance problems and to help capitalize on performance opportunities are in staff functions, such as Human Resources Development (HRD), Data Processing (DP), and Industrial Engineering (IE). That's fine. We cannot expect line managers to be masters of all of the possible performance improvement interventions. However, we have not, in general, carved out the appropriate roles for our staff people. They tend to be perceived (and, often, to perceive themselves) as providers of specific solutions. For example, the HRD folks provide training solutions, the DP people provide computer-systems solutions, and the IE mission is to provide workflow streamlining and ergonomic solutions.

Unlike diagnostically focused doctors, however, our staffers are frequently purveyors of their functions' unique brands of patent medicine, claiming that their potions will cure what ails you. We believe that every staff analyst or consultant, regardless of the breadth of his or her "product line," should be first of all a diagnostician. A dose of performance medication that does not address the disease is at best a waste of money. At worst, it causes side effects more serious than the original affliction.

Ideally, a line manager with a need would conduct a diagnosis and call in representatives of all of the staff functions that can contribute to a comprehensive solution. However, we have found that a line manager generally does not have these skills, any more than a sick person has the ability to diagnose his or her own illness before calling in the appropriate specialist. Line managers have a feeling of pain or opportunity, and they know they need to take some action. However, in our experience, *line managers rarely know what action they need to take to address a performance improvement opportunity*. This reality puts the burden on staff people to diagnose situations before implementing solutions.

The Three Levels Approach to Performance Diagnosis and Improvement

We have found that the Three Levels performance improvement process is an effective way for any staff person to diagnose a situation before recommending action. At the least, it enables the analyst to tailor his or her solution to the organization unit's unique situation. At the most, it may indicate that a solution involving his or her elixir does not address the highest-priority need.

A Situation Requiring Diagnosis

The Vice President of Operations for the partially fictionalized Property Casualty, Inc. (PCI), has requested that Larry Monahan, one of his Procedures Analysts, develop an updated, clearer, and more comprehensive Claims Manual for the organization's Claims Representatives.

Larry will be using the fourteen-step Three Levels approach, which appears in Figure 9.1. As we discuss the application of each step to this situation, we will display some of the forms he may use. However, the process should not be forms-driven and need not be as formal as it's depicted here. The heart of the process is the sequence of steps, the questions that need to be answered at each step, the organization of the information obtained in response to the questions, and the link between actions and diagnosis.

Project Definition and Plan

Step 1: Project Defined. In this step, Larry interviews the Vice President of Operations. His goal is specifically to define the Critical Business Issue

Figure 9.1. The Three Levels Performance Improvement Process.

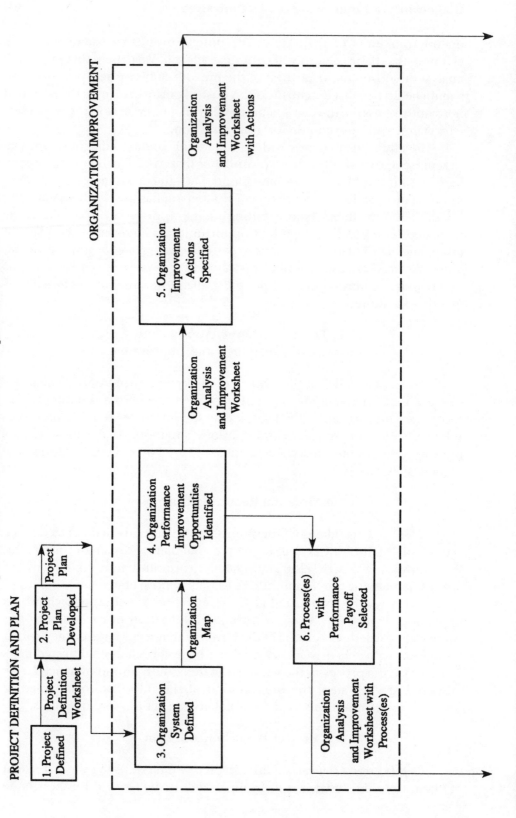

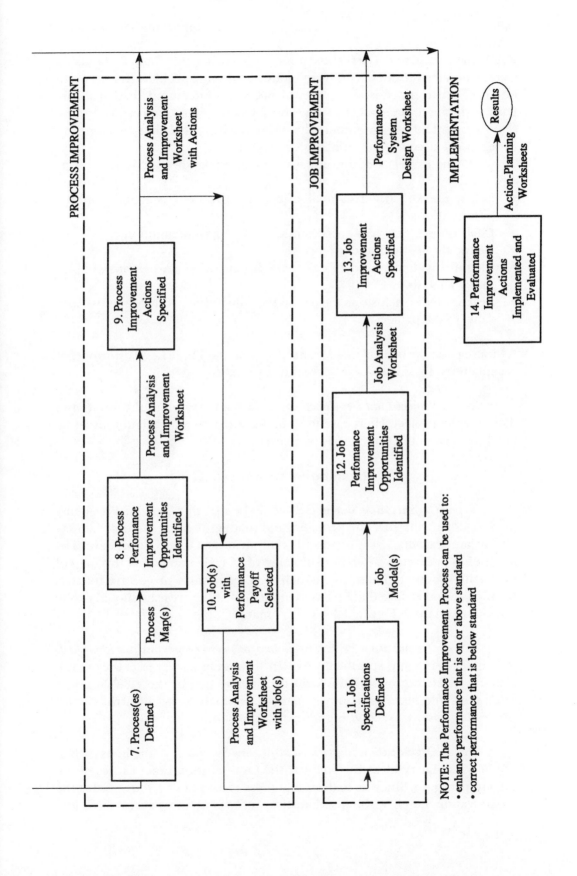

PROCESS IMPROVEMENT

7. Process(es) Defined

Process Map(s)

8. Process Performance Improvement Opportunities Identified

Process Analysis and Improvement Worksheet

9. Process Improvement Actions Specified

Process Analysis and Improvement Worksheet with Actions

10. Job(s) with Performance Payoff Selected

Process Analysis and Improvement Worksheet with Job(s)

JOB IMPROVEMENT

11. Job Specifications Defined

Job Model(s)

12. Job Perfomance Improvement Opportunities Identified

Job Analysis Worksheet

13. Job Improvement Actions Specified

Performance System Design Worksheet

IMPLEMENTATION

14. Performance Improvement Actions Implemented and Evaluated

Action-Planning Worksheets

Results

NOTE: The Performance Improvement Process can be used to:
• enhance performance that is on or above standard
• correct performance that is below standard

(CBI) that stimulated Larry's assignment. Updating the Claims Manual is clearly the Vice President's preferred solution to some problem. If Larry is to be an effective diagnostician, he will need to understand that problem. During the interview, he learns that the Vice President's concern is *excessive claim payouts*. The average amount that PCI is paying per claim is too high and is negatively affecting the company's margins.

During Project Definition, Larry will also take these actions:

- Learn the specific financial effect the problem is having on the organization.
- Establish project goals based on the desired payout amount.
- Define the scope of the project.
- Identify his client and define the roles he and other key persons will play in the analysis.
- Reach some conclusions regarding the constraints, odds of success, and value of the project.

Assuming that the project makes sense, and that the Three Levels approach is acceptable to his client, Larry proceeds to Step 2.

Step 2: Project Plan Developed. In this step, Larry plans the events and dates for the project. He is careful to indicate the data and data sources he needs at each of the three levels of analysis.

Organization Improvement

Step 3: Organization System Defined. To be sure that the Vice President's proposed "fix" will solve the problem, and to identify other factors that may affect claim payouts, Larry begins his analysis at the Organization Level. His first step is to develop a Relationship Map of PCI. He knows that this map of functions, inputs, and outputs will help him see how his project fits into the big picture and ensure that he has identified all of the areas he should probe during his analysis. Figure 9.2 is Larry's map.

Step 4: Organization Performance Improvement Opportunities Identified. In Step 4, Larry wants specifically to identify high-impact gaps at the organization level. He begins with the focus provided to him by the Vice President but is alert to other opportunities. During his analysis, he unearths claims-processing cost as a second high-impact opportunity.

Step 5: Organization Improvement Actions Specified. While he is gathering his data, Larry identifies some of the Organization Level causes of the high-impact gaps. Since he realizes that these causes can be addressed at the Organization Level, without exhaustive analysis at the Process and Job/

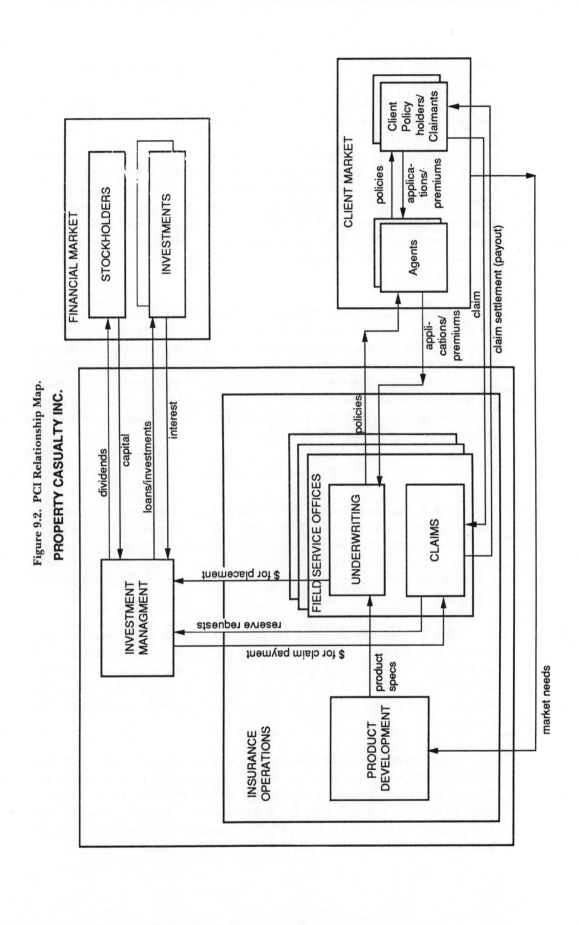

Figure 9.2. PCI Relationship Map.
PROPERTY CASUALTY INC.

Performer Levels, he develops a set of recommended actions to address these causes on the basis of the Three Performance Needs at the Organization Level: Organization Goals, Design, and Management. For example, Larry sees no problem with Organization Goals and Design, but in the area of Organization Management, he learns that the Underwriting and Claims Departments often don't understand the insurance products that come out of Product Development. He recommends vehicles for providing this feed-back to Product Development and for establishing a stronger link between the customer and Product Development. These Organization Level recommendations will be added to those Larry develops at the Process and Job/Performer Levels.

Step 6: Processes with Performance Payoff Identified. To bridge to the Process Level, Larry analyzes the three PCI processes that have impacts on payout amount. He investigates the *underwriting* and *new-product development* processes. While he has no doubt that those processes could be improved, Larry identifies the *claim-handling* process as the one with the greatest impact on the goals of his project. At this point, Larry would update his plan, specifying the steps he will take at the Process Level. Table 9.1 presents a summary of Larry's work in Steps 4, 5, and 6.

Process Improvement

Step 7: Processes Defined. In this step, Larry works with a group of Claims Representatives and Claims Supervisors to construct a Process Map, which depicts the claim-handling process as it should flow. (In many in-stances, this type of group first needs to document the "is" process as a backdrop for the creation of the "should.") Their Process Map appears in Figure 9.3.

Step 8: Process Performance Improvement Opportunities Identified. Hav-ing documented the claim-handling process, Larry identifies the desired performance for each process step, the actual performance, any gaps be-tween desired and actual performance, and the impact of those gaps. He identifies significant gaps in the "claim qualified" and "claim assigned" pro-cess steps.

Step 9: Process Improvement Actions Specified. In Step 9, Larry identifies the causes of gaps revealed in Step 8 and the process improvement actions that will remove the gaps. He limits his list of recommended actions to those that can be taken at the Process Level, without analysis at the Job/Performer Level. Larry finds causes that require clarifying performance expectations and providing feedback.

Table 9.1. PCI Organization Analysis and Improvement Worksheet.

CRITICAL BUSINESS ISSUE: Settlements
ORGANIZATION: Insurance Operations/Claims

ORGANIZATION OUTPUTS (PRODUCTS)	DESIRED PERFORMANCE (STANDARDS)	ACTUAL PERFORMANCE	GAP (IF ANY)	IMPACT OF GAP	CAUSE OF GAP	ORGANIZATION IMPROVEMENT ACTION	PROCESS WHICH INFLUENCES GAP
Claim Settlements	A. Payout/Claim $1500	$1700	$200	$1.8 Million Profit	• Bad specs on New Policies • Policies misrated • Poor measurement of payout performance	• FB to Prod. Develop. on claim perf. • Better input on cust. needs. • FB to Underwriting • Change underwriting objectives. • Better tracking of payout performance	Claim Handling
	B. Time/Claim 60 Days	60 Days	None				
	C. Handling Cost/Claim $215	$375	$160	1.4 Million	• Claims misrouted through agents	• Clarify proper rate for claims and/or • Develop procedures for how agents should process misrouted claims	

Figure 9.3. PCI Claim-Handling Process.

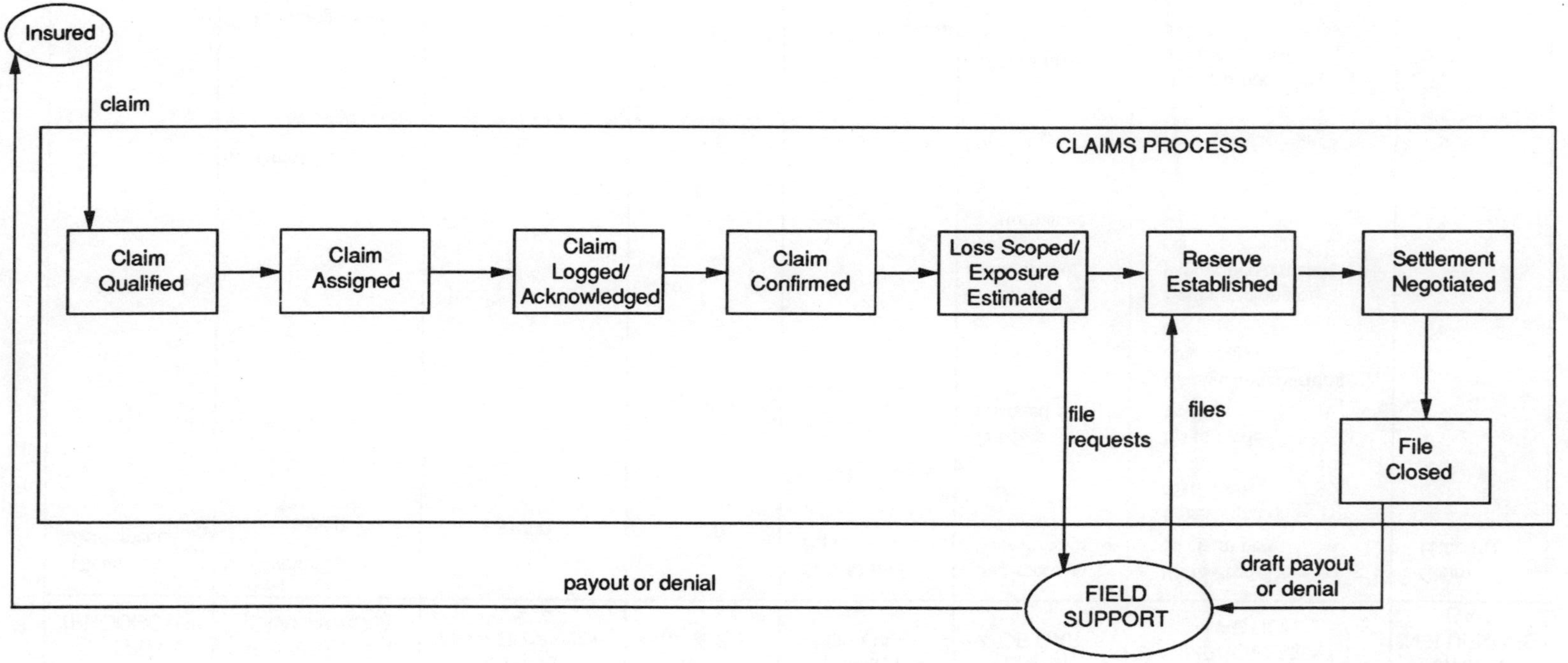

CLAIMS PROCESS

Insured

claim

Claim Qualified → Claim Assigned → Claim Logged/ Acknowledged → Claim Confirmed → Loss Scoped/ Exposure Estimated → Reserve Established → Settlement Negotiated → File Closed

file requests

files

draft payout or denial

FIELD SUPPORT

payout or denial

Step 10: Job(s) with Performance Payoff Identified. As the last step in Process Improvement and a bridge to Job Improvement, Larry identifies the jobs that contribute to the process steps in which there are gaps. His analysis indicates that the Claims Supervisor job—*not the Claims Representative job*—requires the most attention during the Job Improvement phase. Table 9.2 summarizes Larry's work in Steps 8, 9, and 10.

Job Improvement

Step 11: Job Specification Defined. In Step 11, Larry and a group of Claims Supervisors and Managers define the outputs and standards that the "should" process requires of the Claims Supervisor job. Table 9.3 displays a portion of the Job Model that the group creates for the Claims Supervisor.

Step 12: Job Performance Improvement Opportunities Identified. The Job Model produced in Step 11 describes the performance that the Claims Supervisor needs to produce. In Step 12, Larry compares the current performance to the Job Model's standards and identifies gaps, the impact of the gaps, and the causes of the gaps. He uses the Human Performance System (see Chapter Six) to help him identify the causes of gaps. One of his more significant findings is that the Claims Supervisors, when qualifying claims, should identify the recovery potential 75 percent of the time. They are doing this in only 18 percent of the cases. Larry's analysis reveals that Supervisors are not measured, evaluated, or trained in recovery-potential identification. Table 9.4 summarizes some of his analysis for the Supervisor job.

Step 13: Job Improvement Actions Specified. For each gap, Larry develops a recommended gap-closing action. Cognizant of the fact that an effective medicine is one that fits the disease, his action development is focused on the causes of the gaps. A partial picture of Larry's Step 13 is in Table 9.5.

Implementation

Step 14: Performance Improvement Actions Implemented and Evaluated. In this final step in the process, Larry summarizes the recommendations from all three levels of his analysis. He uses the questions associated with the nine Performance Variables (Chapter Three, Table 3.2) as a checklist to make sure his recommendations address the performance needs at all Three Levels. He conducts a cost-benefit analysis on the recommendations and develops a proposed high-level implementation plan. Lastly, he takes his recommendation package through the process that he and the Vice President of Operations agreed on during the Project Definition and Planning phase.

Table 9.2. PCI Process Analysis and Improvement Worksheet.

CRITICAL BUSINESS ISSUE: Settlements
PROCESS: Claims Handling

PROCESS STEPS/ OUTPUTS	DESIRED PERFORMANCE (STANDARDS)	ACTUAL PERFORMANCE	GAP (IF ANY)	IMPACT OF GAP	CAUSE OF GAP	PROCESS IMPROVEMENT ACTIONS	JOBS WHICH INFLUENCE GAP
Claim Qualified	Recovery potential identified on all claims	Not done on 82% of cases on post audit	82%	Cost per claim	No feedback to permit improvement of identification skills / No consequences or feedback to support continued performance where skills are in place	Provide feedback on the outcome of identified cases of potential recovery	Claims Supervisor
	Missing or inaccurate information identified and obtained from agent	Identified in 65% of all cases so requiring	35%	Timeliness Cost per claim	Expectations inconsistently communicated	Clarify and communicate expectations	Claims Supervisor
Claim Assigned	Claim processing method selected minimizes processing cost and payout variation potential	Economic assignment not occuring	No economic basis for assignment	Payout high and increasing			

Table 9.3. PCI Claims Supervisor Job Model.

JOB: Claims Supervisor
JOB PURPOSE: Claims Processing

ACCOMPLISHMENTS SUB-ACCOMPLISHMENTS	CRITICAL DIMENSIONS	MEASURES	STANDARDS
CLAIMS QUALIFIED			
Loss Notice received	Accuracy	% of cases of recovery potential identified	75% of cases of recovery potential identified
Claim type identified			
Coverage determined		% of coverage issues identified later	Additional or corrected coverage issues identified in less than 5% of cases
- recovery potential identified			
- legal trends identified & considered			
Missing / Inaccurate information identified		% of Loss Notices entered in correct claim category	All Loss Notices entered. Loss Notice entries reported by claim category
Claims progress tracked	Timeliness	Average Loss Notice processing/ confirmation time	15 min. per Loss Notice
CLAIMS ASSIGNED			
Economic assignment determined	Accuracy	% of adequate justification of method mix variances greater than 5%	All method mix variances greater than 5% adequately justified
- $ exposure estimated			
- Settlement variance potential estimated		Average size of outside assigned claims	Outside assigned claims $1000 or more
- Method option availability determined		% of cases coinspected/reinspected	10% of cases coinspected/reinspected
REP PROCESS SUPERVISED			
Claim Progress Log reviewed	Volume	# of cases in caseload	- Average caseload - 25 cases
Files reviewed as diaried	Timeliness	Average settlement time	- Average settlement time - 20 working days
Coinspections / Reinspections conducted as scheduled	Accuracy	% of payout variance	- Payout variance on post audit of 10% or less in no more that 2% of audited cases
Rep performance opportunities identified			Any Reps performing below st... identified and appropriate c... action implemented

Table 9.4. PCI Job Analysis Worksheet.

JOB: Claims Supervisor

STANDARDS	ACTUAL PERFORMANCE	GAP	IMPACT OF GAP	CAUSE OF GAP (X)*					
				PS	TI	FB	CONS	K/S	CAP
75% of cases of recovery potential identified	Recovery potential identified in 18% of cases	57%	Cost per claim goes up		X	X	X	X	
Additional or corrected issues identified in less than 5% of cases	Additional or corrected issues identified in less than 3% of cases	None							
15 min. per Loss Notice	15 min. per Loss Notice, Average	None							
All Loss Notices entered. Loss Notice entries reported by claim category	Not Done	No loss data in claim office	Payout increases		X		X	X	
All method mix variances greater than 5% adequately justified	Method mix variances greater than 5% and not justified 8 out of 12 months	Economic Assignment not achieved (or not verified) 75% of processing year	Cost per claim goes up	X		X			
Outside assigned claims $1000 or more	20% of outside claims $500 or less	20% of claims misassigned	Cost per claim goes up				X	X	
10% of cases coinspected/ reinspected	Coinspection/ reinspection in 3% of cases	Quality control sample 7% below requirement	Payout increases						
All Reps performing to the following levels: - Average caseload- 25 working days - Average settlement time-20 working days - Payout variance on post audit of 10% or less in no more than 2% of audited cases	55% of Reps performing to standard Corrective action plans implemented for 50% of substandard performers	45% substandard 50% of substandard not addressed/ supported	Payout increases & cost per claim goes up			X			

* PS = Performance Specifications
TI = Task Interference
FB = Feedback
CONS = Consequences
K/S = Knowledge/Skill
CAP = Capability

Table 9.5. PCI Performance System Design Worksheet.

PERFORMANCE SPECIFICATIONS		TASK INTERFERENCE avoidance/removal	FEEDBACK	CONSEQUENCE	KNOWLEDGE & SKILL	CAPACITY
ACCOMPLISHMENTS	STANDARDS					
	(See Job Model Worksheet and Job Analysis Worksheet)					
Claim Qualified	75% of cases of recovery potential identified	Ensure sufficient time for claim qualification	Provide data on recovery $ from all cases	Evaluate supervision on this aspect of their performance	Develop job aid for claim qualification	
	All loss notices entered	Analyze field support processes		Return notices with errors or incomplete data to agent to fix	Provide training on notice preparation	
Claim Assigned	All method mix variance >5% adequately justified		Determine measurement system and use consistantly to verify economic assignment			
	Assign outside claims $1000 or more		Mgr. evaluation criteria to be based on claim processing cost vs. Rep activity level	Evaluation criteria on performance appraisal	Initiate s[...] trainin[...]	
	10% of cases coinspected					

Summary

At first blush, this process may appear to overkill the assignment. After all, Larry was just asked to update a manual. However, he took it upon himself to get at the problem that had stimulated the request. Through the Three Levels Performance Improvement Process, he identified actions that will result in a far more significant payback than what would have been realized from a better Claims Manual.

This entire process could certainly occupy thirty days of Larry's time. However, we have to examine the output of that thirty-day analysis and compare it to the output of thirty days of manual rewriting. We also need to acknowledge that Larry could have used shortcuts that retained the integrity of the Three Levels approach and significantly reduced the number of work hours and amount of elapsed time.

Larry is an effective "performance doctor." He specifically pinpointed the illness. He thoroughly diagnosed the patient at the Organization, Process, and Job/Performer Levels, and he recommended a treatment that was based on his diagnosis. He has provided an exemplary staff service: the analysis and improvement of line performance.

▰▰▰▰▰▰▰▰▰▰▰▰▰▰▰▰▰▰▰▰▰▰▰▰▰▰▰▰▰

CHAPTER 10

IMPROVING AND MANAGING THE PROCESSES OF THE ORGANIZATION

And that's the way it is.

— *Walter Cronkite*

Processes are "the way it is." In Chapters Two, Three, and Five, we emphasized the importance of recognizing that work gets (or doesn't get) accomplished through processes. Failure to improve process performance results in failure to improve organization performance. Failure to effectively manage processes is failure to effectively manage the business.

A number of large corporations—including IBM, Ford, Boeing, GTE, McDonnell Douglas, Motorola, and AT&T—have implemented Process Improvement and/or Process Management efforts. These statements illustrate the importance that some of these organizations place on managing the horizontal organization:

- "We simply cannot achieve and maintain our goals of leadership in quality, cost, and on-time programs without continuously improving the processes we use to conduct our business.... The resulting quality improvements in process are estimated to represent a significant portion of our cost savings opportunities" (John Manoogian, Ford Motor Company, 1989).
- "[IBM] identified five elements of a total quality improvement system.... One of these brought attention to viewing all work activity as process and ultimately became known as 'quality focus on the business process'" (Edward J. Kane, Director of Quality, Marketing Service and Support Systems, IBM, 1986).
- "All work can be defined as a process...everyone manages a process" (*Process Quality Management and Improvement Guidelines*, AT&T publication, 1987).
- "The key method for achieving...quality improvement goals is the im-

provement of work processes" ("Improving the Process," chapter of Boeing's *Guide to Total Quality*).

Because processes play such a critical role, and because Process Management requires actions that are often countercultural in traditional hierarchies, we believe that the Variables at the Second Level of Performance (defined in Chapter Five) deserve special treatment. However, we believe that maximum-impact Process Improvement projects and sustained Process Management require analysis and action at all Three Levels of Performance.

Steps in Process Improvement

The methodology that follows can be used to fix a broken process, to redesign an existing process in response to a change or in pursuit of continuous improvement, and to design a new process. For simplicity, we will refer to all three applications as *Process Improvement*. A successful Process Improvement project is one in which a cross-functional team addresses a business need by creating an efficient and effective process. The steps in a Process Improvement project are:

1. *Critical Business Issue identified.* Process Improvement begins with senior management's identifying an Organization Level Critical Business Issue (CBI). A CBI is a measurable goal, based on a current or potential problem or opportunity, that has an impact on the strategy of the organization (see Chapter Seven).

A retail store, for example, may have an opportunity to establish a competitive advantage by reducing the time it takes to have the "hot item" of the day available to the customer. Its CBI might be "Reduce order-to-receipt cycle time to two weeks." One of a home security company's strategic objectives may be to close a competitive gap in the area of billing accuracy. Its CBI might be "Reduce the number of billing errors to no more than one error per thousand bills." A chain of pizza parlors may believe it can increase its share of the business-lunch market by speeding up its service. Its CBI might be "Fill customer lunch orders within seven minutes." A manufacturer of home appliances may be losing money on its line of blenders. Its CBI might be "Establish a 10 percent margin in the blender product line."

After the CBI is established, other goals of the Process Improvement effort, if any, are established. For example, top management may want a narrative description of the procedures involved in each process step, an evaluation of the current organization structure, or a set of benchmarking data (documentation of other organizations' process capabilities and characteristics).

2. *Critical Process selected.* Once senior managers have established a CBI, they identify the cross-functional processes that have the greatest potential to resolve it. For the examples just cited, the Critical Processes might be

buying (retail store), billing (home security company), food preparation and customer order (pizza chain), and manufacturing (appliance manufacturer).

3. *Process Team Leader and members selected.* While it may be tempting to assign the task to an analyst, we believe that a successful Process Improvement effort must involve representatives from the functions (departments) that contribute to the Critical Process. The most significant and lasting benefits are derived from the insights and commitment of a sample of the people who will ultimately implement the improvements and work within the process. For example, the functions involved in the Computec order-filling process (see Chapter Five) are Field Operations, Finance, and Production. As a result, an order-filling Process Team should include at least one representative from each of these functions. Each team member should meet these criteria:

- Have a detailed understanding of the process steps in at least one of the functions that contribute to the process.
- Be able to comprehend the big picture (beyond his or her function).
- Not be wedded to the current process.
- Be creative enough to envision a better way of doing things.
- Have a high energy level.
- Be able to work effectively in a peer-group setting.
- Be available to attend team meetings.
- Perceive being assigned to the team as a reward.

A Process Team Leader chairs the team. He or she may ultimately serve as the Process Owner (a term that will be defined shortly). In addition to meeting the criteria for selection as a Process Team member, the Team Leader should be able to effectively manage a task group (establish schedules, control the pace, assign individual tasks, and marshal resources).

We have found that an effective team can be composed of as few as three or as many as twelve members. In most cases, the team is led by a Process Improvement Facilitator whose regular job is not part of the process being analyzed. The Facilitator, who is an expert in using the Process Improvement tools and in leading a group in their use, works closely with the Team Leader. (The Facilitator could learn the necessary skills through several consulting organizations specializing in Process Management.)

4. *Team trained.* The team is taught (usually by the Process Improvement Facilitator) the rationale and tools of Process Improvement.

5. *"Is" Map developed.* The team develops a Relationship Map and a Process Map that describe the current ("is") state. Figure 10.1 displays once again the Computec Relationship Map, which was introduced in Chapter Four. Figure 10.2 reexhibits the Computec order-filling Process Map from Chapter Five.

We have found that the most efficient approach begins with the Process

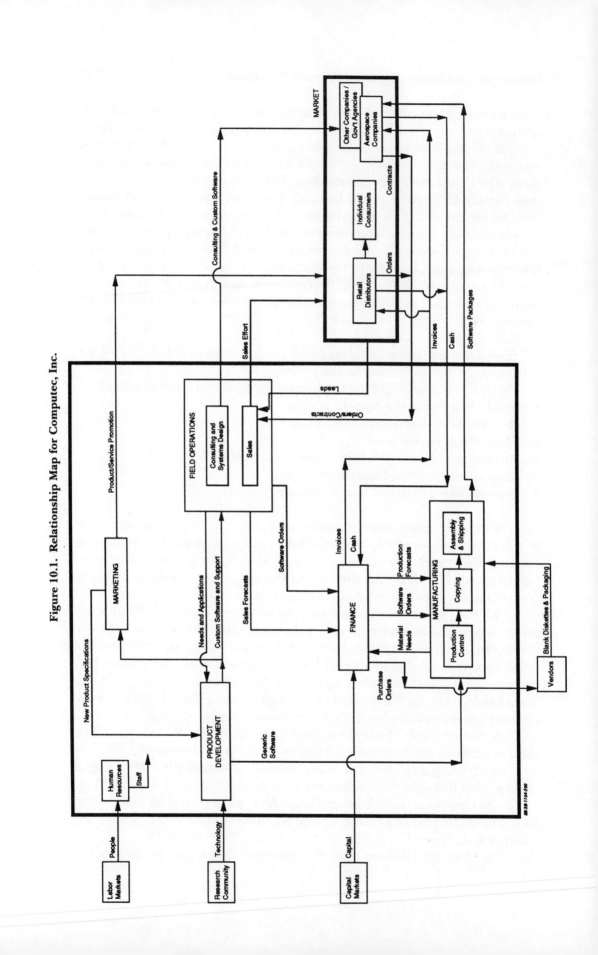

Figure 10.1. Relationship Map for Computec, Inc.

Improvement Facilitator's developing a "straw man" map, based on one-to-one interviews with the team members. When the team first meets as a group, it refines this "straw man," ensuring that it accurately depicts the "is" situation.

6. *Disconnects identified.* As the team is developing the "is" Process Map, it lists the "disconnects" in the process: missing, redundant, or illogical inputs or outputs that could affect the CBI. If, for example, our CBI involves cycle-time reduction, we are particularly interested in disconnects that contribute to wasted time. A second type of disconnect is not a flaw in the logic of the process but rather a failure to efficiently or effectively execute (carry out) a process step. For example, the steps in an order entry process may make sense: however, excessive keying errors result in incorrect orders.

Disconnects are listed but not resolved at this point. Their quality and quantity, along with the definition of the CBI, dictate the appropriate level of detail for the mapping.

7. *Disconnects analyzed.* The full Process Team—or, more commonly, subteams or individuals—identifies the causes of the disconnects. Some causes are already known or not important to the solution. Others require a root-cause analysis technique like fishboning (Ishikawa, 1982) or Kepner-Tregoe problem analysis (Kepner and Tregoe, 1981), to determine why they are occurring. Subteams and/or individuals share their analysis with the full team.

8. *"Should" Map developed.* The team develops a Process Map (and, frequently, a Relationship Map) that depicts a process for achieving the goal of the CBI. This "should" process is a streamlined value chain of activities, which produces the product or service required by the ultimate customer. Since a perfect process may be unaffordable, the Process Team Leader ensures that the team is not being unrealistic in its assumptions about what can be done. Computec's "should" order-filling Process Map appears in Figure 10.3.

9. *Measures established.* Driven by the CBI, the team establishes process and subprocess measures. The first step is to create end-of-line customer measures. (The CBI statement may already contain these.) Then measures with their goals are inserted at critical junctures in the process, as shown in Figure 10.4 (first presented as Figure 5.3 in Chapter Five).

10. *Changes planned, and recommendations developed and presented.* Some Process Teams are empowered to make changes (within certain boundaries) without management's approval. Others need to go through a recommendation process. In either case, the steps required to move from "is" to "should" and to resolve execution disconnects are documented, along with an action plan for their implementation.

At this step, the Third Level of Performance comes into play. If the goals, design, and management at the Job/Performer Level do not support the proposed changes to the process, the improvements will not stick. Frequently, the teams take or recommend these steps:

Figure 10.2. Computec Order Filling: An "Is" Process Map.

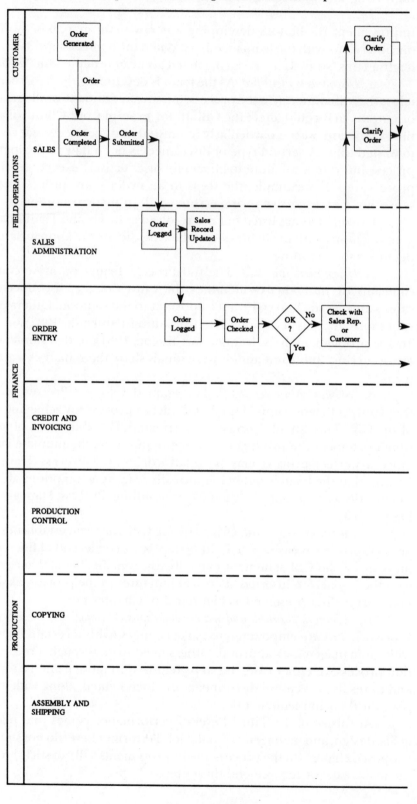

Figure 10.2. Computec Order Filling: An "Is" Process Map, Cont'd.

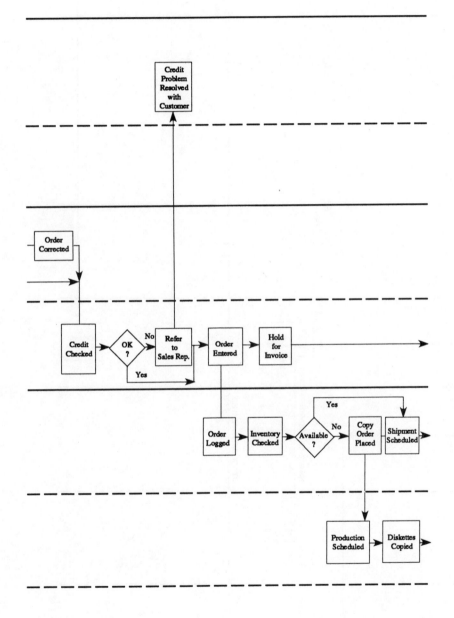

Figure 10.2. Computec Order Filling: An "Is" Process Map, Cont'd.

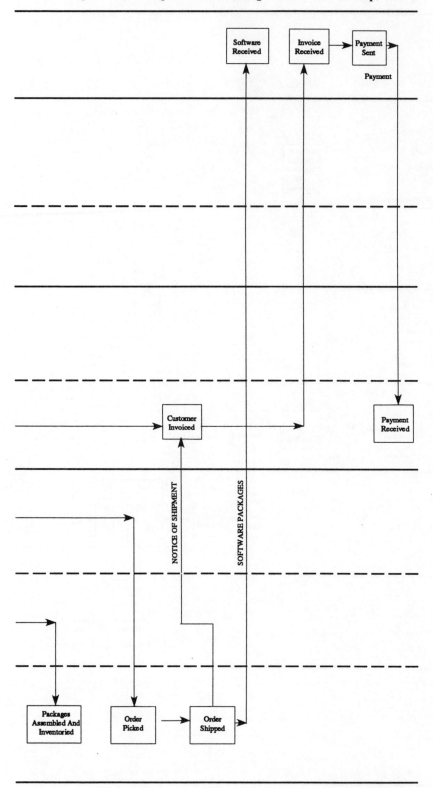

- Adding, deleting, or modifying jobs
- Providing training
- Establishing or modifying reward systems
- Providing additional resources

The Human Performance System variables introduced in Chapter Six—Performance Specifications, Task Interference, Consequences, Feedback, Skills and Knowledge, and Individual Capacity—are a particularly useful guide to planning for change.

11. *Changes implemented.* In this step, the improvements are implemented with the plan developed in Step 10.

How long does a Process Improvement project take? It depends on a variety of factors:

- The nature and magnitude of the CBI
- The other goals of the Process Improvement effort
- The complexity of the process
- The state of the process (a "primitive" process, which has never been documented, measured, or managed, takes more time to analyze and improve than a process that is mature and requires only fine-tuning)

We have participated in Process Improvement projects that accomplished the first ten steps in five half-day meetings on consecutive days. At the other end of the spectrum, we have worked with a massive process in which five subprocess teams met full-time for six weeks over six months. A typical project spans two or three months and involves eight to ten meetings of four to six hours apiece.

Examples of Process Improvement Projects

The following examples represent a sample of Process Improvement projects in which we have participated:

- A team in a computer component manufacturing firm was concerned about its low percentage of on-time delivery. A cross-functional team of twelve managers worked for four days to analyze the entire order-to-delivery process and to make a series of recommendations, which were implemented over a two-month period. This Process Improvement effort resulted in a reduction in average cycle time, from seventeen weeks to five weeks, and a 65 percent increase in on-time delivery. This process continued to be improved during the ensuing twelve months, and cycle time is now down to five days.
- The senior management of a regional telephone company was concerned with the performance of its customer billing process, which involved

Figure 10.3. Computec Order Filling: A "Should" Process Map.

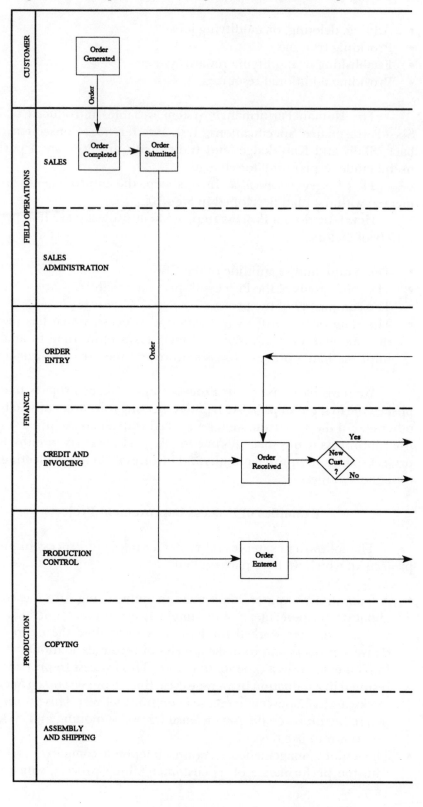

Figure 10.3. Computec Order Filling: A "Should" Process Map, Cont'd.

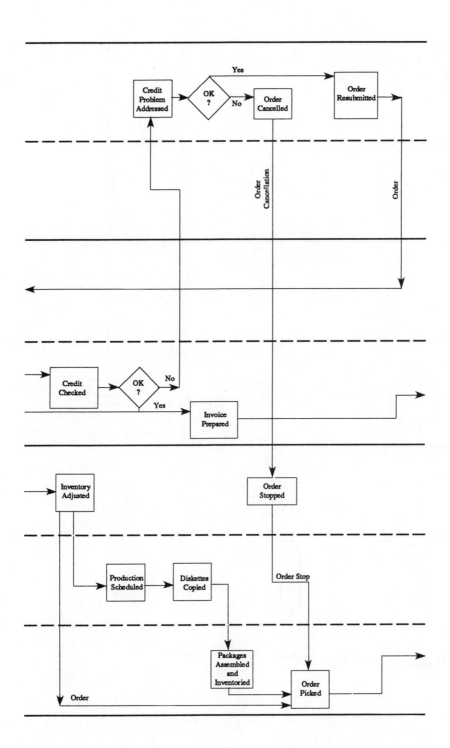

Figure 10.3. Computec Order Filling: A "Should" Process Map, Cont'd.

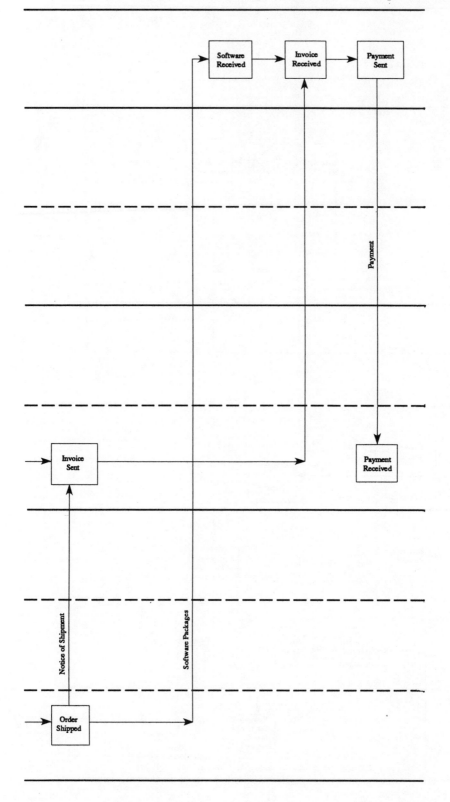

nearly every function in the company. The Process Improvement effort was driven by the need to improve quality in an increasingly deregulated environment. Because of the breadth and complexity of the process, five cross-functional subprocess teams were formed. They found 183 disconnects in the process. Implementation of these improvements resulted in quality gains (based on customer surveys), cost savings, and a measurement system for tracking the contribution each function made to the overall process.

- Three midlevel peer managers were under severe competitive pressure to significantly reduce the time their company took to design and develop a new communications product and get it into high-volume production. They initiated a cross-functional Process Improvement project in which a team of twelve managers and engineers worked for five days. They analyzed the "is" process and developed a "should." The new process has reduced product development and introduction from thirty-six to twelve months. New products proceed through the process under the watchful eye of a process oversight committee, which consists of the three managers who initiated the project.

- A new telecommunications company was considering a growth-through-acquisition strategy. The Chief Executive Officer and his top management team used mapping to document their entire sales-to-invoice process. They then broke into subgroups, each of which responded to a different scenario in which the organization acquired a company with certain characteristics. Each group used the Map to identify the potential process problems and opportunities presented by that type of acquisition, as well as the Process Improvement actions that would be essential to the successful integration of the new company. This analysis was a major input to their acquisition decisions and to the implementation of their growth strategy.

- A consumer products company was undergoing a reorganization that involved two new Vice Presidential positions and new roles for three existing Vice Presidents. To clarify these new responsibilities, the President and the Vice Presidents met for three days during one week. Using a map of their organization, the team decided how the organization would process three different types of orders and how the annual plan would be put together. The result was clarification of and agreement on the role of the major functions. They also identified and subsequently resolved issues that probably would have impeded the reorganization. This *proactive* use of Process Improvement enabled them to minimize "white space" problems in the new organization.

- A new division President in a large insurance company, along with his field and home-office staffs, used mapping as a tool for clarifying field and home-office roles in making, implementing, and monitoring policy and in troubleshooting field problems. One of the significant benefits of

Figure 10.4. Selected Process Subgoals for Computec Order-Filling Process.

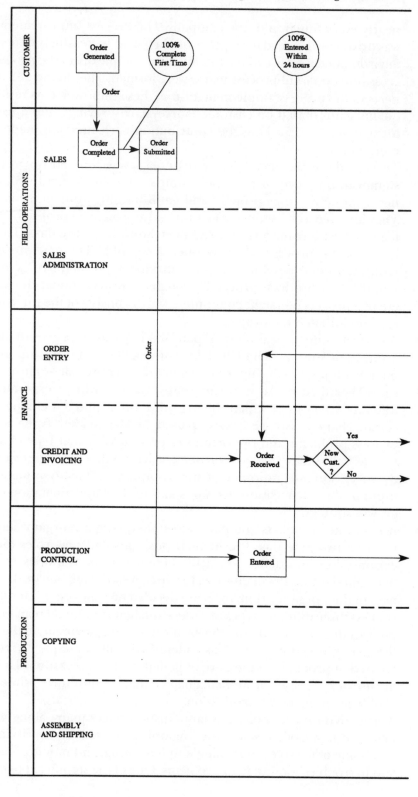

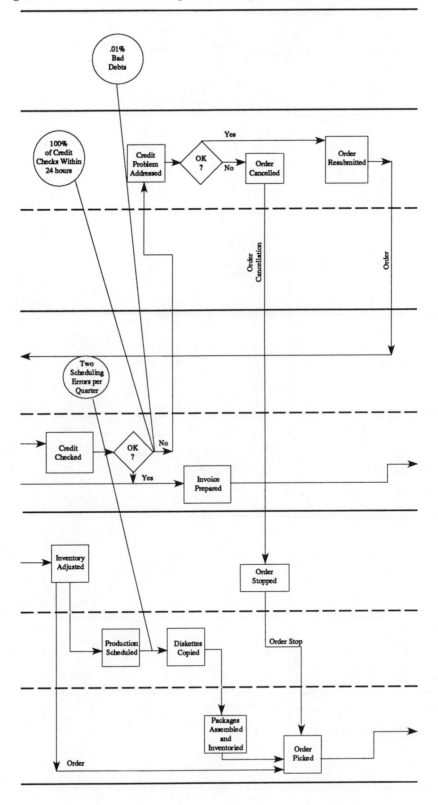

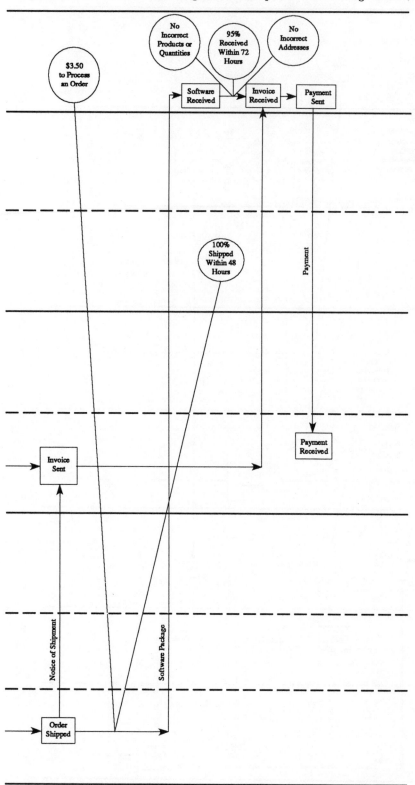

their one-day meeting was the President's comprehensive understanding of the flow and functional relationships within his new division.

- An engineering and manufacturing firm was concerned about the flood of Japanese patents. The patent application process in this company took an average of two years, *before* the application was even submitted to the U.S. Patent Office. By analyzing and improving the process, a team was able to immediately reduce the time to six months, and it continues to improve.

- A task force in a high-technology company began its design of its semi-conductor "factory of the future" at the Organization Level, by specifying the goals and general parameters of the factory. The members then used "should" Process Mapping (Level II) to design the production process and the key support processes. Lastly, they moved to Level III and identified the jobs, skill sets, and staffing required by the processes.

Not all of these projects religiously followed the eleven Process Improvement steps. Each, however, involved a cross-functional team, using mapping and other Process Improvement tools, to address a Critical Business Issue. The foregoing examples include all four uses of Process Improvement:

- Solving a current problem (billing quality)
- Improving a process that is basically satisfactory but has room for improvement (customer service)
- Evaluating and implementing a change (acquiring a company)
- Designing a new system (the "factory of the future")

Process Management

Step 11 in a Process Improvement project is not the end; it's the beginning. If an infrastructure for the ongoing management of a process is not established, the process will fall into disrepair as quickly as a rebuilt car engine that is not kept tuned. Process Management is a set of techniques for ensuring that key processes are continuously monitored and improved. Figure 10.5 includes the four steps (boxes) that precede and the all-important step that follows Step 11. As Figure 10.5 shows, senior managers' involvement in the first three steps ensures that they understand Process Improvement and Management; participate in the planning for the initial project, including the selection of the issue, process, and key players; and commit to providing a supportive environment for the effort.

Selecting Strategic Processes. While a long-range goal may be to establish a Process Management plan for every process, most organizations begin by identifying the critical few processes that warrant the investment in

Figure 10.5. Elements of a Successful Process Management Effort.

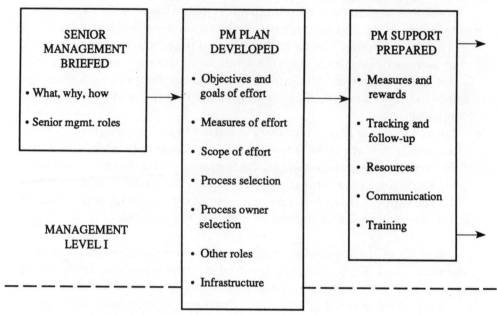

Figure 10.5. Elements of a Successful Process Management Effort, Cont'd.

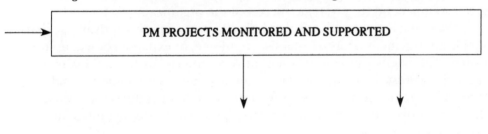

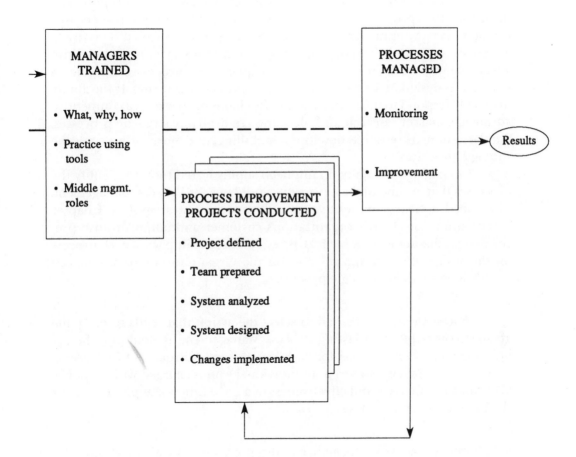

ongoing Process Management. These processes are those that have the greatest impact on the strategic success of the organization.

A strategic process is one that influences a competitive advantage that senior management wants to establish, reinforce, or expand. For example, if order-cycle time is a potential competitive advantage, order processing is a strategic process. If the quality of customer service is a competitive advantage, the customer service process is strategic. If new products are central to the competitive advantage, product development and product introduction are strategic processes.

These examples of strategic processes are all customer processes (processes that produce a product or service visible to the customer; see Chapter Five). Administrative (purely internal) processes can also be strategic. For example, if the cost of producing a product or service is a competitive advantage, the budgeting and capital expenditure processes may be as strategic as design, material management, and manufacturing. If the ability to quickly respond to the needs of a rapidly changing market is a competitive advantage, market research and planning are probably strategic processes. Similarly, human resource development, billing, and purchasing could be strategic processes.

Top managers usually do not need sophisticated tools to identify the processes that are the highest-priority candidates for Process Management. They need a clear, competitive advantage–driven strategy (see Chapter Seven) and a list of their organization's customer and administrative processes (see Chapter Five, Table 5.1). By evaluating the impact of each process on the competitive advantages and on the Organization Goals, they can readily identify their strategic processes.

Process Owners. If we had to select the action that tends to make the greatest contribution to lasting Process Management, it would be the appointment of a *Process Owner* for each key process. A Process Owner (sometimes called a *Process Sponsor*) is an individual who is charged with responsibility for the efficiency and effectiveness of a cross-functional process. He or she plays some or all of these roles:

- Monitors process performance and reports periodically to senior-management about how well the process is meeting customer requirements and internal goals, as well as about any indications that the process is being suboptimized
- Ensures that a permanent Process Team continuously improves process performance
- Serves as a "white-space ombudsman," who facilitates the resolution of interface problems among the functions that contribute to a process
- Develops a process plan and budget

- Serves as the conscience and champion of the process
- Evaluates and certifies the process

Without a Process Owner, the "white spaces" tend to be ignored. As each line manager manages his or her piece of the process, functional optimization or process suboptimization (described in Chapter Two) is likely to occur.

Like a matrix manager, who oversees the cross-functional performance of a product or a project, the Process Owner oversees the cross-functional performance of a process. Unlike a product or project manager, however, the Process Owner does not represent a second organization structure. Individuals are not continually torn between their commitments to their vertical (line) and horizontal (product or project) managers. In effective Process Management, reporting relationships remain vertical; the functional managers retain their power. The horizontal dimension is added if the functional managers are judged by their departments' contributions to one or more processes and if Process Owners ensure that interface problems are resolved and that process considerations dominate functional interests. There is one more distinction between a Process Owner and a product or project manager: products and projects come and go; processes are permanent.

Given this pivotal role, the selection of the Process Owner is critical. While not all of these characteristics are essential, a Process Owner tends to be someone who:

- Holds a senior management position
- Holds a position that gives him or her major equity in the total process (the most to gain if the process succeeds, and the most to lose if it fails)
- Manages the largest number of people working in the process
- Understands the workings of the entire process
- Has an overall perspective on the effect the environment has on the process and the effect the process has on the business
- Has the personal ability to influence decisions and people outside his or her line-management responsibility

The Process Owner's responsibility is usually associated with the position, rather than with an individual. For example, we worked with a telephone company in which the Vice President of Finance was appointed Process Owner for the billing process. When he left that position, his successor became the Process Owner.

We were initially surprised by the low level of conflict between effective Process Owners and the managers of the functions that contribute to the processes. We believe that good Process Owners do not threaten line managers, because they are doing things that nobody has done before. They are adding value without taking anything away from other managers.

Institutionalizing Process Management

In an organization that goes beyond Process Improvement projects and institutionalizes Process Management, each key process has:

- A map that documents steps and the functions that perform them
- A set of customer-driven measures, which drive functional measures (see Chapters Five and Eleven) (in an institutionalized Process Management environment, functions cannot look good against their measures by hurting other functions and the process as a whole)
- A Process Owner
- A permanent Process Team, which meets regularly to identify and implement process improvements
- An annual business plan, which includes the key process's expected results, objectives, budget, and nonfinancial resource requirements
- Mechanisms (such as process control charts) for the ongoing monitoring of process performance
- Procedures (such as root-cause analysis) and vehicles (such as Process Teams) for solving process problems and capitalizing on process opportunities

To ensure that processes meet these and other performance criteria, IBM, Ford, and Boeing have established process certification ratings. To achieve the top rating on a four-point scale a Ford process must meet thirty-five criteria. These criteria range from the need for the process to have a name and be documented to a requirement that the process be assessed by customers as free of defects. The Process Owner takes primary responsibility for administering the evaluation and certification process.

Institutionalized Process Management is not just a set of certified processes. It is also a culture in which:

- Process Owners, Process Teams, and line managers practice continuous process improvement, rather than sporadic problem solving.
- Managers use their Relationship and Process Maps as tools for planning and implementing change, orienting new employees, evaluating strategic alternatives, and improving service to their internal and external customers.
- The needs of internal and external customers drive goal setting and decision making.
- Managers routinely ask and receive answers to questions about the effectiveness and efficiency of processes within their departments and about cross-functional processes to which their departments contribute.
- Cross-functional teamwork is established through the enhanced under-

standing of other departments, the streamlining of interfaces, and the compatibility of goals.
- Optimum process performance is reinforced by the Human Performance Systems in which people work (see Chapter Six).

When Process Management is institutionalized in an organization, the systems view (see Chapter Two) is the framework for addressing performance problems and opportunities. Process effectiveness and efficiency are the end to which policy, technology, and personnel decisions are means.

Managing the Vertical and Horizontal Organizations

Institutionalization of Process Management requires the peaceful co-existence of the vertical and horizontal dimensions of an organization. In most cases, a purely horizontal organization structure (organized solely around processes) is not practical. It is often more efficient for people in Finance, Human Resources, and Systems to be grouped together.

How does an organization establish effective vertical and horizontal structures? In our experience, the key is measurement. More about this subject will be said in Chapter Eleven, but here we can say that establishing customer-focused, process-driven measures is the first step. In a process-driven environment, each functional manager is still responsible for achieving results, allocating resources, and developing policies and procedures. *The only difference from a traditional (purely vertical) organization is that each function is measured against goals that reflect its contribution to processes.* Line managers have as much authority as in any traditional organization. There is no tug-of-war between two bosses, as in many matrix-managed organizations.

A department always contributes to the greater good. In an institutionalized Process Management environment, that greater good is the processes that serve the organization strategy. Because Process Management fosters symbiotic, "we're all in this together" relationships between suppliers and customers, functional managers may need assistance in managing the "white space." That assistance is available from the Process Owner.

In summary, Process Management can coexist quite peacefully with the functional organization because:

- It doesn't change the direction of the business.
- It doesn't (necessarily) change the organization structure or reporting relationships.
- It ensures that functional goals are aligned with process goals.
- It doesn't change accountability or power.
- It changes how the business is conducted only because it ensures that processes (which are there already) are rational.

The Role of Top Management

An organization does not have to implement Process Management all at once. A top manager who is interested in Process Management should begin by instituting a couple of Process Improvement projects. If these projects successfully resolve Critical Business Issues, he or she should consider institutionalizing Process Management, at least for the organization's strategic processes. A top manager's role in institutionalization may include:

- Identifying strategic processes
- Appointing or serving as a Process Owner
- Appointing permanent Process Teams
- Asking and requiring answers to the questions behind all nine of the Performance Variables
- Using process measures as the foundation for performance evaluation, rewards, and troubleshooting
- Chairing a Process Owner panel that conducts process reviews, which are similar to traditional operations reviews
- Installing and managing a process planning system, which resembles typical business planning
- Ensuring that the work environment (rewards, feedback, resources) supports process effectiveness and efficiency

Process Improvement and Management and the Three Levels of Performance

Effective Process Improvement is not limited to the Process Level of Performance. Process Improvement projects with the greatest impact begin with the identification of a Critical Business Issue associated with a key process. Issue and process identification should be based on strategic goals at the Organization Level. Process Improvement cannot take root if it is limited to the Process Level. All system enhancements have to be reflected in the jobs and the environment at the Job/Performer Level.

Similarly, ongoing Process Management is not just management of the Process Level. An ongoing assessment of Organization Level needs should direct the Process Management priorities. In addition, a cornerstone of Process Management is the monitoring and improvement of the Job/Performer Level. To manage the performance of a process, one must manage the performance of the people who work within that process. To manage people's contributions to process effectiveness, one must manage the variables of the Human Performance System—Performance Specifications, Task Interference, Consequences, Feedback, Skills and Knowledge, and Individual Capacity.

Summary

Process Improvement projects systematically improve the Process Level of Performance, which serves as the link between the strategic goals of the Organization Level and the Job/Performer Level at which those goals will ultimately be carried out. Process Management involves establishing an infrastructure for the ongoing management and improvement of key processes. Process Improvement and Management reap "hard" benefits (such as the resolution of Critical Business Issues and the improvement of systems) as well as "soft" benefits (such as enhanced cross-functional teamwork and the establishment of a customer-focused, continuous-improvement culture). In our twenty-five years in the performance improvement business, we have found no other tool whose impact is as profound and lasting as that of Process Improvement and Management.

▗▄▄▟▀▀▀▀▙▄▄▖▗▄▄▟▀▀▀▀▀▀▀▟▄▄▟▀▀▀▀▙▄▄▄▄▟▀▀▀▀▀▀▟▄▄▄▖

CHAPTER 11

MEASURING PERFORMANCE
AND DESIGNING
A PERFORMANCE
MANAGEMENT SYSTEM

If performance isn't being measured, it isn't being managed.
— Unknown

The selection of measures and the related goals is the greatest single deter-
miner of an organization's effectiveness as a system. For example, one organization we encountered, which manufactured and distributed paint to
independent dealers, was losing money and market share. Its basic work flow
was quite straightforward: Sales representatives took orders from paint dealers. These representatives placed the orders with their Regional Distribution
Centers, which then supplied the paint to the dealers. Distribution Centers
replenished their stock by ordering paint from Manufacturing.

During a discussion with the new division president, we discovered
that:

- Sales representatives were measured (and compensated) on the basis of
  their bookings (orders).
- Distribution Centers were measured on the basis of "lines per load,"
  which was the extent to which a truck or boxcar was full before it
  departed.
- Manufacturing was measured on the basis of "yield," which was the
  amount of paint produced per production line.

If each of these functions—Sales, Distribution, and Manufacturing—is
viewed in isolation (in its own "silo"), the measures make sense. However, let's
look at the effect of these measures on the performance of the business. As a
result of the Distribution Center measurement system, product ship dates
were determined by when the truck or car was full rather than by when the
customer needed the product. The result was delays in filling orders. As a
result of the Manufacturing measurement system, large amounts of a product

were produced (so that yield could be optimized) before the lines were switched to another product. Frequently, a Distribution Center needed its stock replenished to meet current orders at a time when Manufacturing was producing a different product. The result, again, was delays in filling orders. In this situation, internal efficiency measures overrode customer satisfaction measures. Who suffered from this measurement system? Initially, the customers did. Ultimately, it was the company.

All organizations start with an almost overwhelming network of financial measures in place. Add to that measures driven by past problems, shifting emphases of new managers, and new corporate programs of quality, cycle time, and customer service. The result is a collection of largely unrelated and unmanageable measures, leading in many cases to "measurement gridlock" — managers in a state of paralysis because they can't move performance affecting one measure in a positive direction without (seemingly) moving two other measures in a negative direction.

We discuss measurement in our treatment of goals and management at the Organization (Chapter Four), Process (Chapter Five), and Job/Performer (Chapter Six) Levels of Performance. However, we believe that measurement is *the* pivotal performance management and improvement tool and, as such, deserves special treatment.

Without measures, we don't get the desired performance. With the wrong measures, we suboptimize organization performance. As you will see, the Three Levels framework enables us to move from gridlock to identification of the "critical few" measures, from a mere collection of measures to a measurement system. The result is the ability to manage all the variables that affect organization performance.

Why Measure?

We have established that an organization is a system and that there are Three Levels of Performance — Organization, Process, and Job/Performer — that must be managed in order to get consistent, high-level organization output. *We measure so that we can monitor, control, and improve system performance at all three levels*, as shown in Figure 11.1. (In Figure 11.1 and throughout this chapter we show measurement points in the system as meters.)

Without measures, *managers* have no basis for:

- Specifically communicating performance expectations to subordinates
- Knowing what is going on in their organizations
- Identifying performance gaps that should be analyzed and eliminated
- Providing feedback that compares performance to a standard
- Identifying performance that should be rewarded
- Effectively making and supporting decisions regarding resources, plans, policies, schedules, and structure

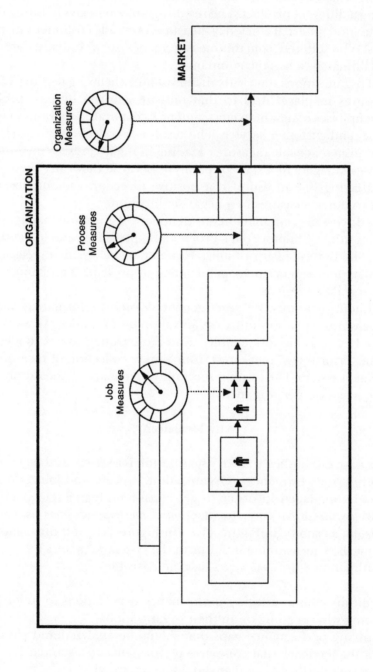

Figure 11.1. Measuring the Three Levels of Performance Within the Organization System.

Without measures, *employees* at all levels have no basis for:

- Knowing specifically what is expected of them
- Monitoring their own performance and generating their own feedback
- Generating their own rewards and understanding what performance is required for rewards from others
- Identifying performance improvement areas

Requirements for Effective Management of the Organization System

Merely establishing measures is not enough; for the organization system to be effectively managed, it is necessary that:

1. We have sound measures that ensure that we are monitoring the right things
2. There be a total measurement system, not a collection of unrelated — and potentially counterproductive — measures
3. There be a performance management process that converts the data provided by the measurement system into intelligent action

Based on our experience, we would like to suggest some guidelines in each of these three areas.

Developing Sound Measures

What we want to measure is performance — that is, output — at all Three Levels. Regardless of the Level (Organization, Process, Job/Performer) we recommend that measures be developed following this sequence:

1. Identify the most significant outputs of the organization, process, or job.
2. Identify the "critical dimensions" of performance for each of these outputs (see Gilbert, 1978). Critical dimensions of *quality* include accuracy, ease of use, novelty, reliability, ease of repair, and appearance. Critical dimensions of *productivity* include quantity, rate, and timeliness. Critical dimensions of *cost* include labor, materials, and overhead.

    Critical dimensions should be derived from the needs of the internal and external customers who receive the outputs and from the financial needs of the business.
3. Develop the measures for each critical dimension. For example, if "ease of use" has been identified as a critical dimension of quality for a given output, one or more measures should answer this question: "What indicators will tell us if our customers find our product or service (output) easy to use?"
4. Develop goals, or standards, for each measure. A goal is a specific level of

Table 11.1. Examples of "Sound Measures."

Outputs	Critical Dimensions	Measures	Standards
Insurance Claims Qualified	Accuracy	% of cases of Recovery potential identified	75% of cases of Recovery potential identified
		% of coverage issues identified later	Additional or corrected coverage issues identified in less than 5% of cases
		% of Loss Notices entered in correct claim category.	All Loss Notices entered. Loss Notice entries reported by claim category
	Timeliness	Average Loss Notice processing / confirmation time	15 min. per Loss Notice
Orders Taken	Accuracy	Number accurate orders / total	100%
	Timeliness	By specific time	Within 2 minutes

performance expectation. For example, if a measure for ease of use is "number of customer questions/complaints regarding product use," a goal may be "no more than two questions/complaints per month." As continuous improvement efforts bear fruit, goals should become more ambitious.

Table 11.1 shows several examples of measures developed in this way. Important characteristics of this approach to developing measures are:

1. They are output-driven. This is in contrast to the frequent practice of settling on goals and measures because they are topical or easy to measure rather than because they will help achieve a critical output.
2. They are customer-focused: The outputs, critical dimensions, and goals are all determined to a substantial degree by customer requirements.
3. They reflect the reality that most outputs have several critical dimensions and that measures must be multidimensional in many cases. We can no longer get away with thinking that "we can have quality or we can have quantity, but we can't have both." We can have both, as well as "timeliness." That is the new customer requirement.

Ideally, every measure and goal/standard is developed following this sequence.

Building a Measurement System

Organization effectiveness comes about only when the Organization, Process, and Job/Performer Levels are all headed in the same direction. The key to this is a measurement network that ties the Three Levels together into a system. Such a measurement system makes it possible:

1. To monitor performance at all levels and "troubleshoot" failure. For example, a deficient organization level output can be tracked back to a faulty process and process step and a missing or faulty job output, where corrective action can be taken
2. For all performers along the chain to see and measure their impact on the critical organization outputs

    The process of building the measurement system requires two stages:

1. Establishing the output linkage from Organization output to Process output to Job/Performer output (Our mapping technique is particularly helpful in this stage.)
2. Overlaying relevant measures on these outputs following the "sound measures" sequence described above

    To illustrate how a measurement system can be built let us re-examine Computec, the software and systems integration company we used as our example in Chapters Four, Five, and Six.

    Organization Level. The development of the measurement system starts at the Organization Level, determining the critical outputs and goals. One of Computec's strategic goals was to "capture 60 percent of the aerospace project management market within three years."
    Because goals at the Organization Level drive all other measurement, it is particularly critical that they:

*   Are based on the documented requirements of the external customer and the strategic business requirements of the organization
*   Are universally understood within the organization
*   Reflect the organizationwide performance to which all subsystems (processes, departments, and jobs) should contribute

    Process Level. The first step in linking Process measures to Organization measures is to link the Organization output to the Process Level outputs. In the case of Computec, the organization output is "project management software." However, management realizes that the key to penetrating this particular market and achieving the market share goal is the introduction of a series of new project management software products. Therefore, a process critical to achieving this Organization Level goal is the new product development process. Computec's first step in determining process measures is to put into place a new product development process. Following the procedure

Figure 11.2. Computec Product Development and Introduction:
"Should" Process Map and Sample Goals.

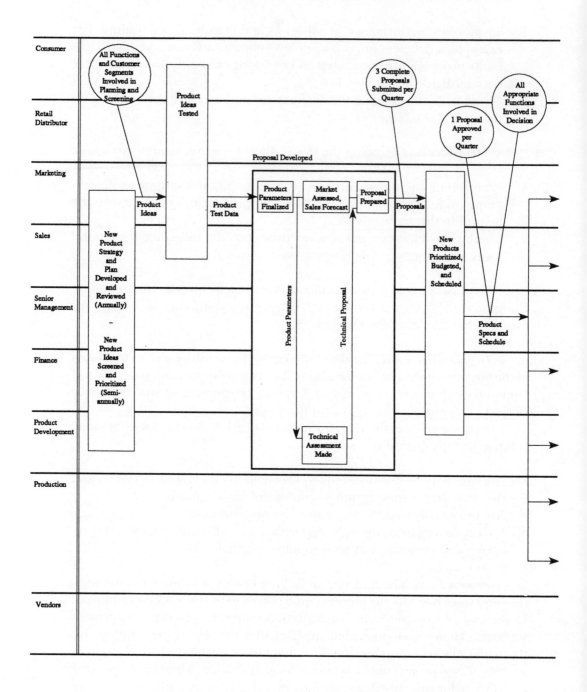

Figure 11.2. Computec Product Development and Introduction:
"Should" Process Map and Sample Goals, Cont'd.

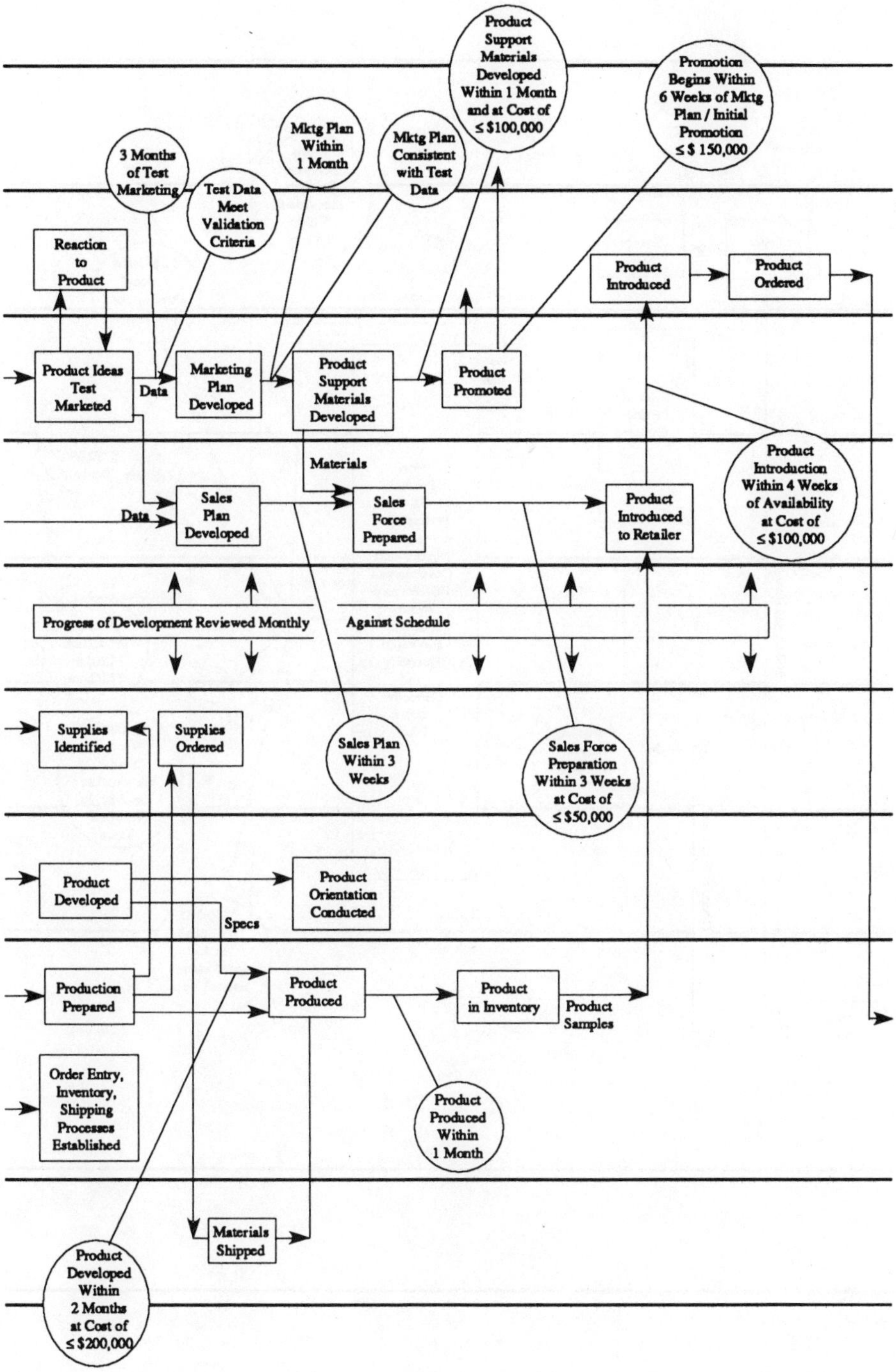

Figure 11.2. Computec Product Development and Introduction:
"Should" Process Map and Sample Goals, Cont'd.

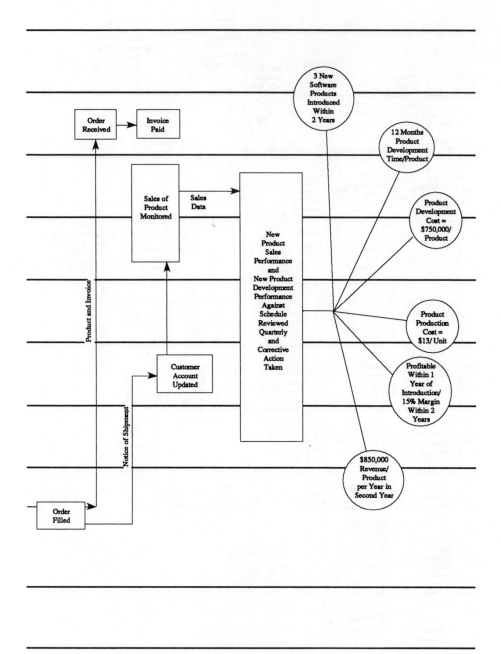

Figure 11.3. Output Measures.

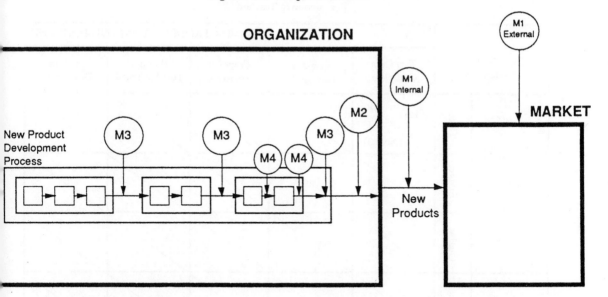

outlined in Chapter Ten, Computec has developed a "should" new product development process, shown in Figure 11.2. This process map is really an output chain showing the output links from process step to subprocess to final process output.

Once we have established the output links, we can overlay the appropriate measures, as shown in Figure 11.3. M (meter) 1 measures organization performance. There can be both M1–External measures relating directly to customer requirements and M1–Internal measures reflecting customer requirements as well as organization business requirements (for example, "60 percent of the aerospace project management market within three years" for Computec). M2 measures end of process (new product development process) performance. M2 measures are related to the M1 measures, either internal or external or both. (In the case of Computec, the M2 measures for new product development process performance include "three new software products introduced within two years.") M3 measures the outputs at each subprocess point and M4 measures the outputs of process steps (if necessary). This network of measures (1) is customer and business strategy driven and (2) allows for monitoring and troubleshooting process performance as it affects the desired organization output.

Referring to Figure 11.2, we can see how this would actually look for the Computec new product development process. Included in Figure 11.2 are the end of process goals (M2) and a sample of some upstream (subprocess—M3—and process step—M4) goals. These measures and goals should have been developed following the proposed "sound measures" sequence. Thus we have linked the critical outputs and built a measurement system linking the Organization Level to the Process Level.

Table 11.2. Computec Product Development and Introduction:
Performance Tracker.

Product Idea		MAJOR PRODUCT DEVELOPMENT AND				
		Test Data Complete	Proposal Developed	Proposal Approved	Product Test Marketed	Product Developed
"Eagle"	Time	(Plan) / (Actual)				
	Budget					
	Quality					
"Cardinal"	Time					
	Budget					
	Quality					
"Hawk"	Time					
	Budget					
	Quality					

Table 11.2. Computec Product Development and Introduction:
Performance Tracker, Cont'd.

INTRODUCTION PROCESS STEPS					
Product in Inventory	Product Promoted	Sales Force Prepared	Product Introduced	Product Shipped (First 1,000 Units)	Initial Revenue Target Met

Once the Process Goals are established, senior management — especially the Process Owner — needs a vehicle for tracking the performance of the process. (Process Owners are covered in Chapter Ten. The Computec Vice President, Marketing, most likely would be the Process Owner for product development and introduction.) A simple tracking format appears in Table 11.2.

Linking Process and Function/Department Measures and Goals. If the Process Goals displayed in Figure 11.2 are to be the primary drivers of function (department) performance, Computec has to be sure that each function's measures reflect:

- Its contribution to overall process (and, in turn, organization) goals
- The contribution it needs to make to other functions so that they can make *their* contributions to process and organization performance

The Process Map format makes it easy to see the contribution each function is expected to make to the process. The meters that fall within each band become the measures/goals for that function. Figure 11.4 shows how the Process Map can be extended to reflect the goals for each function that contributes to the product development process. These goals can serve as the basis for allocating human and financial resources.

If we managed the Marketing Department, for example, and if the Marketing row in Figure 11.4 were complete, we would clearly understand the contribution we were expected to make to the product development process, how that contribution would be measured, our specific goals for a current product development effort, and the resources we could use to meet those goals.

A tool we have used frequently in complex processes (such as product development) is the "Role/Responsibility Matrix." This Matrix translates the Process Map into a set of responsibilities for each contributing department. By displaying the responsibilities in this format, we can increase the likelihood that no process steps fall between the cracks, that there is no overlap, and that everyone understands who does what. Table 11.3 displays a portion of a Role/Responsibility Matrix for Computec's product development and introduction process. (A Process Role/Responsibility Matrix such as shown in Table 11.3 is a different format for displaying the data contained in a cross-functional map. Such a Matrix has added value only if a process is very complex or the cross-functional map was not developed in sufficient detail.) While Table 11.3 does not include goals, you may find it useful to include them in the Matrix.

Marketing undoubtedly supports a number of processes besides product development and introduction. It also carries out responsibilities that are not in direct support of a major cross-functional process. Table 11.4 shows a portion of a Marketing "Function Model" that would enable its management to track the department's overall contribution to the organization.

The Job/Performer Level. Computec's top managers can ensure that the Organization and Process Levels drive day-to-day performance by cascading the goals down to the Job/Performer Level. The first step in that process is to allocate each department's outputs (which were derived from process requirements) among the various jobs in that department. A function Role/Responsibility Matrix, which is an extension of the Process Role/Responsibility Matrix (Table 11.3), helps organize and display these outputs. Table 11.5 shows how the Marketing Department's outputs could be distributed among jobs in that department.

Each column in the department's Role/Responsibility Matrix becomes the set of outputs required of the people in a job. At the Job Level, "outputs" are the accomplishments of individuals who contribute to a function/process output. From the perspective of the function or the process, they are suboutputs. If (as is typically the case) a job supports more than one process, the incumbents' total job responsibility would include the outputs listed under their job title in all Role/Responsibility Matrices.

For the final "job description," we use a format called a "Job Model." A Job Model, which is an extension of the Role/Responsibility Matrix, contains not only the job's outputs but also the measures and goals for each output based on the function measures and goals. (Note that a Job Model directly incorporates the format for developing "sound measures.") Table 11.6 is a portion of a Job Model for the Research Analyst in Computec's Marketing Department.

The Job Model represents the final link in a measurement system that ties the Organization Level output to the individual output. Such a measurement system provides a "line of sight" from the individual to the organization output and makes it possible for management to effectively monitor and troubleshoot system performance.

We realize that we have presented quite a few worksheets. Figure 11.5 shows their relationship.

Using Measures as the Foundation of a Performance Management System

Most managers do not have an effective measurement system that encompasses all Three Levels of Performance. And those who do have appropriate and comprehensive measures usually fail to take the next step, which is to use the measures to effectively manage performance. For example, we developed a measurement system for a manufacturing plant that had been performing poorly for some time. The plant manager held daily production meetings, which, due to the inadequate quality and quantity of information available to all levels of management, had historically been

Figure 11.4. Computec Product Development and Introduction:
"Should" Process Map and Sample Functional Goals.

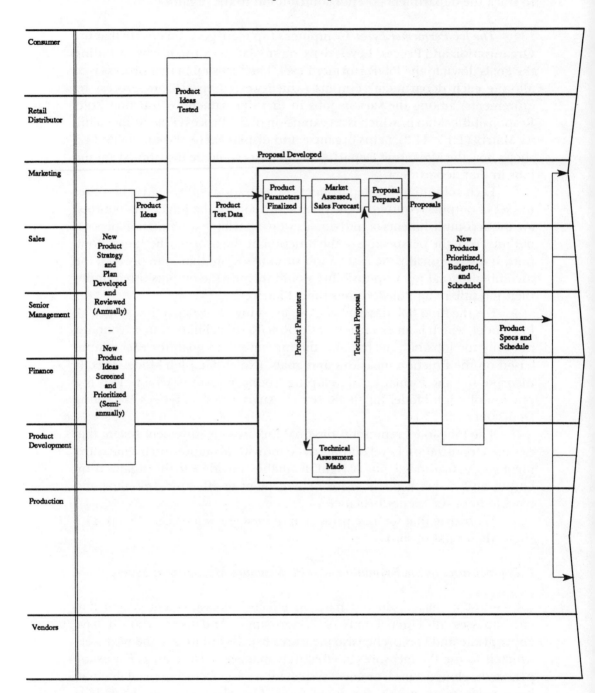

**Figure 11.4. Computec Product Development and Introduction:
"Should" Process Map and Sample Functional Goals, Cont'd.**

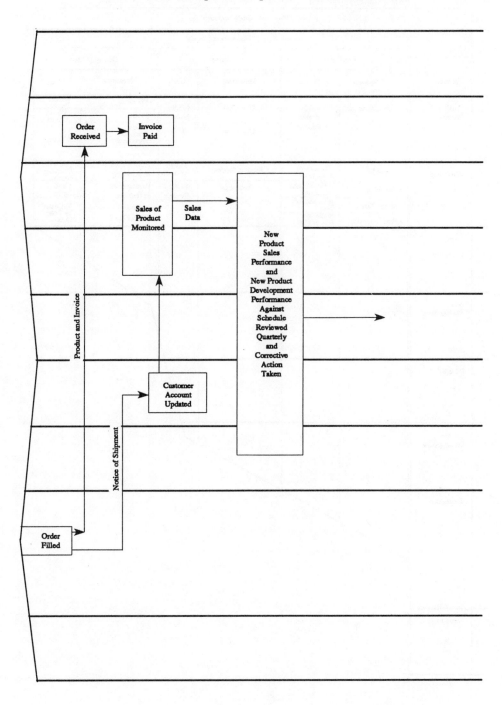

Figure 11.4. Computec Product Development and Introduction: "Should" Process Map and Sample Functional Goals, Cont'd.

Functional Goals Summary						
	Measures and Goals					
	Timeliness		Budget		Quality / Other	
Function	Measures	Goals	Measures	Goals	Measures	Goals
Total Process	Dev. Time	12 Months/ Product	Dev. Cost	$750k/ Product	• Revenues	$850k/ Product
					• Profit	15% w/i 2 Years
			Unit Cost	$13/ Unit	• # New Products Introduced	3 in 2 Years
Marketing	• Proposal	4 Weeks After Idea	Product Support	$100k/ Product	Participation in Screening	100% of Customers/ Depts.
	• Test Mktg.	3 Mo. of Data Gathering	Promotion	$150k / Product	Participation in Decision	100% of Depts.
	• Mktg. Plan	w/i 1 Mo. of Test				Validated by Test Data
	• Prod. Support	Matls. w/i 1 Mo. of Plan			Mktg. Plan	
Sales						
Senior Management						
Finance						
Product Development						
Production						
Vendors						

Table 11.3. Role/Responsibility Matrix for the Computec Product Development and Introduction Process.

Major Process Steps	Functions And Responsibilities				
	Marketing	Sales	Senior Management	Finance	Product Development
1. New Product Ideas Screened & Prioritized (Semi-Annually)	• New Product Ideas Solicited and Formatted for Formal Review • Discussion, Evaluation, & Prioritization of Ideas Facilitated	• Product Ideas Submitted • Ideas Evaluated, Prioritized	• Product Ideas Submitted • Ideas Evaluated, Prioritized	• Ideas Evaluated, Prioritized	• Product Ideas Submitted • Ideas Evaluated, Prioritized
2. Product Ideas Tested	a. Product Evaluation Questionnaire Prepared c. Consumer and Distributor Participants Jointly Selected for Product Evaluation d. Evaluation Conducted e. Test Data Summarized f. Test Data Revised and Product Ideas Selected for a Development Proposal	b. Evaluation Questionnaire Reviewed			
3. Product Proposal Developed	a. Product Parameters Described For Technical Review c. Market Size Evaluated and Marketing and Sales Strategy Articulated For Each Product. Marketing & Sales Cost & Time Evaluated e. Sales Estimates and Break-even Point Established For Each Product f. Proposals Finalized			d. Product Development Cost Estimates Developed	b. Product Technical Feasibility Assessed & Cost & Time Estimates Developed

Table 11.4. Portion of the Computec Marketing Function Model.

Function Model			Dept. Marketing	
			Period 1/1 – 12/31	
I. Process Support				
Process	Function Outputs/ Accomplishments	Critical Dimension	Measure	Goals
Product Development & Introduction	• Proposal Written	Timeliness Budget Quality	Dev Time	12 Hours
	• Market Tested			
Market Research	• Market Plan Written			
Promotion				
II. Non-Process Support				
Category	Function Outputs/ Accomplishments	Function Measures/Goals		
General Support	• Inquiries Handled			
	• Tours Conducted			
Special Projects	• Corporate Brochure Updated			
	• Customer Conference Managed			

frustrating finger-pointing sessions. When presented with the first information generated by the new measurement system, the plant manager said, "This is great! Now I know exactly who the S.O.B. is that has been screwing up. I'll have his butt in the next production meeting." This response represents a typical management misuse of a measurement system.

Table 11.5. Role/Responsibility Matrix for the Computec Marketing Function: New Product Development and Introduction.

Major Process Steps	Marketing Function		Marketing Jobs & Responsibilities		
	Outputs	Goals	Research Analyst Outputs	Product Manager Outputs	Vice President, Marketing Outputs
1. New Product Ideas Screened & Prioritized	New Product Ideas Solicited And Formatted For Formal Review	• Ideas Solicited From All Depts/Customer Segments • Review Format Follows Guidelines • Review Each 3/1 & 9/1	• New Product Ideas Solicited From Sales, Software Design, & Product Managers • New Product Ideas Formatted For Review By Process Team		
	New Product Idea Screening, Evaluation, Prioritization Facilitated	• All "Go" & "No Go" Evaluations Supported By Rationale • Priorities Consistent w/ Strategic Needs • Final Screening w/i 4 Weeks of Review			• NP Process Team Convened • New Product Ideas Presented • New Product Ideas Reviewed and Prioritized With Team
2. Product Ideas Tested	Product Evaluation Questionnaire Prepared	• Questionnaire Meets Validity Guidelines	• Questionnaire Designed	• Criteria For Questionnaire Developed Questionnaire Reviewed	
	Study Participants Selected (Jointly With Retail Sales)	• Participants Represent All Constituencies		• Questionnaire Reviewed	
	Evaluation Conducted	• All Participants Agree With Decisions • Evaluation w/ Budget	• Participants Invited to Participate	• Candidates Generated And Reviewed With Retail Sales • Final Participant List Negotiated	

Table 11.6. Portion of a Job Model for the Computec Market Research Analyst.

Marketing Department		Market Research Analyst			
Outputs	Goals	Outputs	Critical Dimensions	Measures	Goals
New Product Ideas Solicited And Formatted For Formal Review	All Departments Formally Polled Semi-annually For Product Ideas	Product Idea Questionnaires Developed And Administered	Quality – Completeness	% of Customers and Departments Included in Distribution	10% of Customers In Each Market Segment 100% of Depts.
			Quality – Ease of Use	# of Complaints/ Queries Regarding Questionnaire Items	∅
			Productivity – Timeliness	Frequency of Questionnaire Distribution	Each March 1st and September 1st
			Cost	$ Per Survey	$15,000
		Questionnaire Responses Consolidated Into Potential Product Report	Quality – Completeness	% of Ideas Included in Report	100%
			Quality – Understandability	# of Complaints/ Queries re: understanding of Report	2 / Report
			Productivity – Timeliness	Time Between Survey and Report	4 Weeks

Another example is the hotel chain for which we were building a management information and performance appraisal system. A district manager checked into one of the hotels in his district late one evening and was extremely irritated when he observed that the ashtrays in the lobby were not clean, per company regulations. The next morning at breakfast, the district manager lectured the hotel manager about the quality of housekeeping in general and particularly about the ashtrays in the lobby. The hotel manager interrupted the breakfast of the housekeeping supervisor and passed on the message from the district manager, with an appropriate level of amplification. The housekeeping supervisor raced to the lobby and cleaned up the ashtrays.

In both of these cases, it is safe to say that the manager's reactions to the performance data (formal reports in the case of the plant manager and

Figure 11.5. A Three Levels Performance Measurement/Management System.

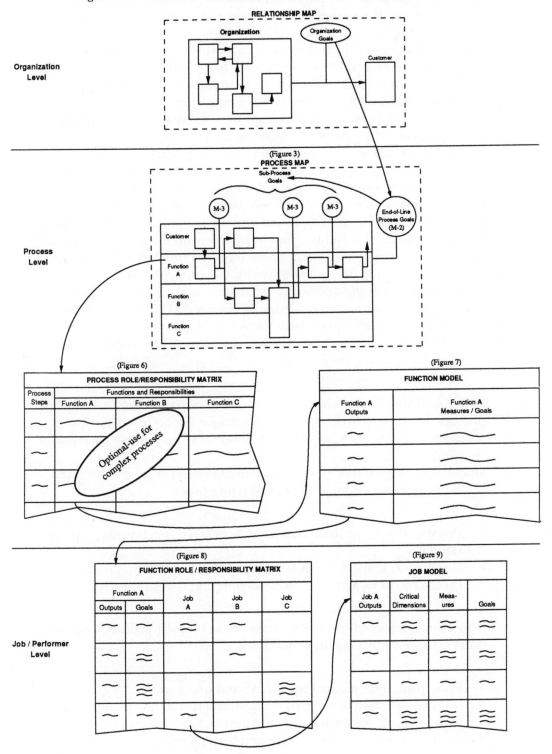

informal observation on the part of the district manager) will enhance neither the performance of their subordinates nor, in the long run, that of their organizations.

The plant manager intends to use the information to affix blame and punish offenders. As a result, managers at all levels will be quick to blame others. Avoiding blame will become more important than delivering products. When we pointed this out to the plant manager, he said, "What do I do? This is the only way I know how to manage." We worked with the manager to design an agenda for the production meetings and coached him in question asking. The focus of the daily production meetings changed from "butt kicking" to problem solving. Over the next three months, the more effective use of performance information enabled the plant manager to reduce the length of production meetings from two hours to thirty minutes. More significantly, the plant accomplished a miraculous turnaround in quality and productivity. Thus, the way information from a measurement system is used is as critical as the nature and extent of the information. Rather than being used to punish, it should be used to answer the question, "Why?"

The second case illustrates two additional side effects of misusing performance information—the tendency of managers (1) to manage behavior rather than results and (2) to drop down a level and do the job of their subordinates. Rather than triggering the chain of events described earlier, the hotel district manager should have:

1. Interpreted the dirty ashtrays as an indication that the housekeeping process might have broken down. The major concern of the district manager should be the state of the housekeeping process, not a particular ashtray.
2. Shared the "dirty ashtray" observation with the hotel manager and asked him some questions about the housekeeping process:

    *   Do you think the housekeeping process is performing up to standards?
    *   How do you know if the process is performing up to standards?
    *   Do the two of us agree on housekeeping standards or goals?

3. If necessary, reviewed the status of the housekeeping process with the hotel manager by asking these questions:

    *   Is the procedure manual up to date and being used?
    *   Is process performance being tracked, and is that information being used for problem solving and decision making?
    *   Are the necessary tools in place and being used?

Based on these data, the district manager might need to take appropriate corrective action with the hotel manager.

4. Suggested that the hotel manager meet with the housekeeping supervisor to determine where the housekeeping process had broken down, leading to the dirty ashtrays. They should have jointly answered these questions:

- Are there deficiencies in the process or the process measures?
- Are we inadequately executing the process? If so, are housekeepers properly trained? Do they have sufficient resources?
- Is the housekeeping supervisor properly managing the process?

Based on the answers, the hotel manager should take appropriate action to prevent the problem from happening again.

In both of these cases, the issue is the intelligent use of measurement data to enhance performance.

A Performance Management System. If we want to effectively manage performance at the Job Level, we need to:

Step 1: Define for the job holders the expected job outputs and levels of performance for each (goal setting).

Step 2: Ensure that the job holders are able to monitor their own performance on an ongoing basis and, if off-target, to diagnose the situation and take corrective action. In addition, the supervisors and managers of that job holder should be able to track critical components of the job/process and troubleshoot off-target performance. However, we want to stress that the job holders should not have to rely on their supervisors/managers for their performance data. It should come directly to them, allowing them to make the necessary adjustments.

Step 3: See to it that the job holders and supervisors/managers periodically (quarterly or semiannually) review performance. This review should be a recap of the frequent discussions between the job holders and managers (described in Step 2), with a focus on performance trends. There should be no surprises for the job holders during this formal review, which should result in a summary performance evaluation and in decisions regarding:

- Action required on the part of the job holders *and* managers to improve performance of the job
- Promotability of the job holders
- Change in compensation for the job holders

- Training and development the job holders need to improve their performance on the current job and/or prepare them for promotion to a new job
- Changes in the goals for the next performance period

If we have these three components, we have the basics of a *Performance Management System*, as shown in Figure 11.6. The goals are set periodically and jointly by job holders and their managers. Performance is monitored, "troubleshot," and corrected continuously by job holders and periodically by their managers. For example, sales representatives should constantly be monitoring, diagnosing, and improving their performance as they call on prospects. Their sales managers should monitor the sales and sales activity information continuously. When the managers travel with the reps every other week, they should observe performance, discuss their observations, and make recommendations for improvement.

The performance improvement component (Step 3) should be performed periodically, resulting in longer-term improvement actions, rewards for the job holders, and goals for the next period.

To effectively manage performance, an organization will have a performance management system for all levels of performers, as shown in Figure 11.7. Relating back to our hotel management example, the division manager sets regional goals with the region manager, who sets district goals with hotel managers, and so on. The objective will be interlocking the job levels, assuring that all job levels in the organization are working toward the same organization goals. The measurement information monitored at each level is determined to a large degree by the outputs required at each level. Each level of management is monitoring key indicators of the subordinate operation, troubleshooting, and suggesting corrective action. Each level of management periodically reviews performance of the subordinate operation against the goals set in Step 1 and determines jointly with the subordinate manager what action is required to continuously improve performance. Such a system will guard against the misuse of measures and enhance the power of measures in these ways:

1. The performance-planning/goal-setting component clarifies the outputs expected from each level. As a result, managers are less likely to do their subordinates' jobs. To ensure support of cross-functional process performance, top management should review this hierarchy of outputs to ensure that responsibilities are linked at appropriate levels throughout the organization. A process for establishing this output hierarchy at all job levels was a major part of the performance management system we developed for the hotel chain described earlier. The system of Role/ Responsibility Matrices, Function Models, and Job Models discussed

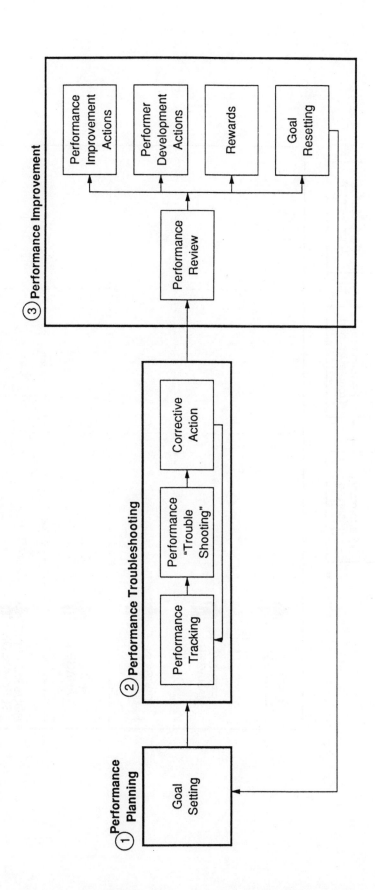

Figure 11.6. Performance Management System.

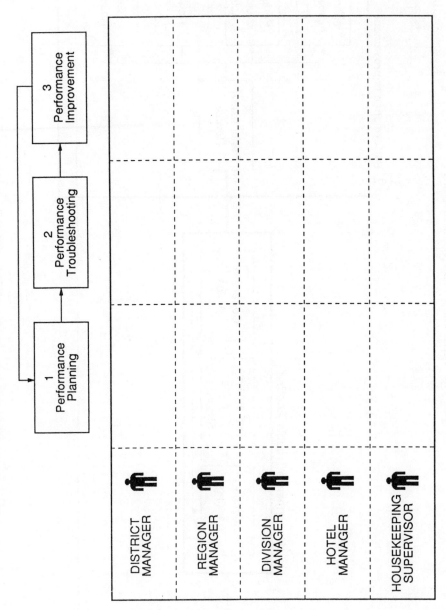

Figure 11.7. Components of an Organization Performance Management System.

earlier in this chapter (see Figure 11.5) is an effective way to determine and display desired job outputs.

2. The measurement system discussed earlier in this chapter provides the information that is tracked in the performance troubleshooting component of the system. The job outputs and goals identified in Step 1 determine to a large degree what measurement information (Step 2) should be available to each job holder. The thrust of this component of the Performance Management System is problem solving and continuous improvement. This is the proper objective of the production meetings of the plant manager and the field visits of the hotel district manager.

3. Performance review and improvement (Step 3) focus on evaluation of results in those *output* areas identified in Step 1. Although various measures are tracked for troubleshooting purposes, formal evaluation should be directed to the achievement of output goals for the period.

A measurement system ensures that measures are interlocked at all Three Levels among all departments and at all levels of performers within each department. A performance management system provides a structure for using measures to effectively manage performance.

Summary

Measurement is the key ingredient in Performance Management. Although the topic is large enough to merit its own book, we have limited our discussion to some areas particularly germane to managing organizations as systems.

We believe that the following "truths" about measurement underlie effective management of organizations and human performance:

- Without measurement, performance isn't being managed.
- Without measurement, one cannot specifically identify, describe, and set priorities on problems.
- Without measurement, people cannot fully understand what is expected of them.
- Without measurement, people cannot be sure whether their performance is on or off track.
- Without measurement, there cannot be an objective, equitable basis for rewards (such as raises, bonuses, promotions) or punishments (such as disciplinary action, downgrading, dismissal).
- Without measurement, there are no triggers for performance improvement actions.
- Without measurement, management is a set of uneducated guesses.

The bad news is that establishing good measures is not easy. The good news is that straightforward techniques and criteria (some of which are provided in this chapter) can help ensure that the quality and quantity of measures meet the needs of both managers and individual contributors.

Measures alone are not enough. Even the right measures are not enough. To serve as guides and tools, measures have to serve as the foundation of a Performance Management *System*. The components of such a system are described above.

The only barrier to Performance Management is lack of willingness to invest the necessary time in building a Performance Management System. While this investment is not insignificant, our experience has shown that it is more than justified by the short- and long-term payback. In Chapter Thirteen, we present a "managing organizations as systems" scenario that shows the benefits of measures-based Performance Management.

▗▄▟▖▗▄▟▖▗▄▟▖▗▄▟▖▗▄▟▖▗▄▟▖▗▄▟▖▗▄▟▖▗▄▟▖

CHAPTER 12

DESIGNING
AN ORGANIZATION
STRUCTURE
THAT WORKS

Had I been present at the creation, I would have given some useful
hints for the better ordering of the universe.

—Alfonso X

American management tends to manage by organization structure. Prevailing wisdom suggests that if an executive can just get the right boxes on the chart, array them in the appropriate hierarchy, and appoint strong people to head them up, the organization will succeed. Toward this end, most large companies embark on a significant reorganization at least once a year.

In Chapter Two, we discussed the advantages of seeing an organization from a process perspective, rather than from an organization structure perspective (see Figures 2.1 and 2.3). The distinction between the horizontal view and vertical view is critical when redesigning organizations. The objective of a reorganization is to improve the performance of the organization. However, organization performance is in most cases a result of the effectiveness of the cross-functional processes (the horizontal system). Therefore, the goal of most reorganizations should be to improve the effectiveness and efficiency of the horizontal organization. This suggests that a reorganization should follow a two-step process:

1. Analyze and redesign the horizontal system—the critical cross-functional processes—so that it will meet customer requirements and organization goals.
2. Redraw the organization boundaries (redesign the reporting relationships) to support the effectiveness and efficiency of the horizontal system.

In effect, form should follow function.

Unfortunately, many reorganizations are carried out with attention

only to the vertical view—the reporting relations—without a real understanding of the needs of the horizontal system. The worst case result is that
the reorganization ends up optimizing the performance of some function
and suboptimizing the horizontal system and the performance of the organization. The best case result is that the restructuring inadvertently benefits the
horizontal system. But the need for the horizontal system to be effective is too
important to leave to chance. Organization Design means just that. If we want
the organization to work, we must design it to do so. And the design work
begins with the understanding of the requirements of the cross-functional
processes or horizontal system. Work gets done through processes; processes
should drive organization structure.

     We also believe that Organization Design (one of our nine Perfor-
mance Variables) should not start or finish with the organization chart.
Organization Design should include:

- A structure at the Organization Level that defines the input-output
  (supplier-customer) relationships that should exist among functions
- A structure at the Process Level that defines the steps through which
  inputs should be converted to outputs
- A structure at the Job/Performer Level that defines individual and work-
  team responsibilities and the environment in which they should be
  carried out

Let us examine a series of steps for developing an organization structure
that works because it encompasses and addresses all Three Levels of
Performance.

Designing an Organization Structure

     We believe that an effective organization structure results from the
following activities and decisions. In the next section, we provide a comprehensive example that illustrates these steps.

     Step 1: Establish a Clear Strategy. Your organization's structure should
facilitate the achievement of its strategy. If an organization has no strategy,
any structure will do. Chapter Seven outlined an organization's strategic
decisions, which include product and service definition, customer and market definition, competitive-advantage identification, and, resource-allocation
priority determination. Once these decisions establish a direction, executives can begin to design a structure that will help take the organization down
that path.

     Step 2: Document and Analyze the Current ("Is") Organization System.
Using a Relationship Map (see Chapter Four), display the inputs and outputs

that connect the current departments in the organization. Identify any "disconnects" (missing, redundant, or illogical connections), especially those that affect the organization's ability to achieve the strategy.

For example, we worked with a small telecommunications company that identified its ability to rapidly introduce new products as one of its competitive advantages. When it developed its "is" Relationship Map, it became clear that it did not have a series of relationships (a process) through which products could be efficiently developed and introduced. Furthermore, Product Development, while it still appeared on the organization chart, was a department that had recently been the victim of a cost-cutting campaign, and it had no staff—hardly a structure through which the strategy could be achieved!

Step 3: Document and Analyze the Current ("Is") Processes. Using Process Maps and cross-functional Process Teams (see Chapters Five and Ten), describe the current flow of the customer and administrative processes that have the greatest impact on the strategy. Note any disconnects that currently or potentially weaken competitiveness.

For example, we worked with an aerospace company whose executives determined that they wanted to capitalize further on a current competitive advantage—their ability to substantially customize their product to meet unique customer requirements. A team constructed a map of the process through which customer options became incorporated into products. It revealed significant disconnects which resulted in confused customers, missed delivery dates, and small or negative margins.

Step 4: Develop "Should" Process Flows and Measures. Use the Process Map format to develop "should" flows for the strategically significant processes analyzed in Step 3. These "should" processes ought to remove the disconnects identified in the "is" processes. Then establish a set of process measures, following the format outlined in Chapter Eleven. At this step, you may have to design "should" subprocesses (further breakdowns) and support (staff) processes.

Step 5: Design the Organization Chart. On the basis of the "should" Process Maps, determine the most logical departmental groupings and reporting relationships. The goal is to draw organization boundaries that maximize process effectiveness and efficiency. There is no formula for drawing the boundaries. The process flow normally suggests a number of workable alternatives. The criteria for selecting the structure that will best serve the process—and, in turn, the strategy—include:

Figure 12.1. Relationship Map of a Traditional Calculator Company.

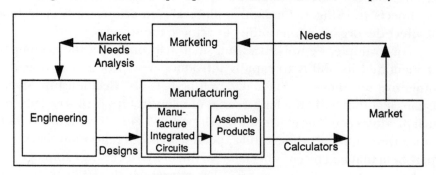

- Maximum product and service quality
- Maximum responsiveness to customers' needs (maximum flexibility and minimum cycle time)
- Maximum efficiency (minimum rework and minimum cost)

To meet these criteria, the organization structure should have:

- The minimum number of interfaces necessary to achieve the quality goals of the process
- Maximum proximity of internal customers and suppliers
- An optimum span of control (number of direct reports per manager)
- A minimum number of layers of management
- Maximum clarity (few if any overlapping or fuzzy responsibilities)

To verify the viability of the organization structure, develop a "should" Relationship Map that eliminates the disconnects identified in Step 2. This Relationship Map may suggest a refinement of the organization chart and will serve as a key input to the Function Models to be developed in Step 6.

The system in a traditional 1970s calculator manufacturing company is displayed in the Relationship Map that appears in Figure 12.1. The Calculator Division of the Casio Corporation decided that it could establish its speed of new-product introduction as a competitive advantage. Its strategy was to dominate the market by introducing a new calculator every six months (compared to the industry average of every two years). The high-level Casio Relationship Map appears in Figure 12.2.

The major boxes on Casio's new organization chart were the same. However, the role of each function, and the organization chart within each function, changed significantly. By changing the role of Marketing and by buying rather than making its integrated circuits, it could establish its new-product introduction process as a competitive edge.

Once you have finalized the organization chart, you can implement the

Figure 12.2. Relationship Map of Casio Calculator Division.

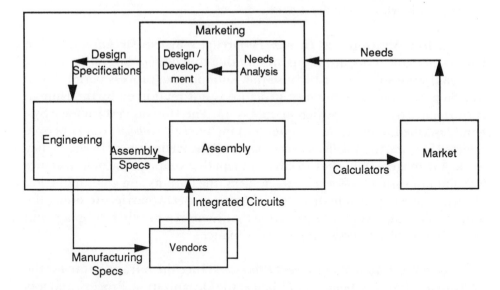

new structure through the Organization, Process, and Job/Performer Levels, as described in the following three steps.

Step 6: Develop Function Models for Each Department. Using the format and rationale provided in Chapter Eleven, define each function in the organization (each box on the new chart) in terms of its outputs and goals. These Function Models should be derived from the Relationship Map's outputs and from the critical *process* outputs and goals. They should describe the responsibilities with enough detail to:

- Clearly and thoroughly communicate each function's role in the organization
- Ensure that function outputs do not overlap
- Ensure that all process outputs and measures are reflected in function responsibilities
- Serve as a firm foundation for the development of Job Models (see Step 7)

We have found that a Role/Responsibility Matrix, which ties each function's key outputs to the steps in a critical process, can provide a useful backdrop for the development of Function Models.

Step 7: Develop Job Models for Each Job. Identify the outputs and goals required from each job in the new organization, using the Job Model format introduced in Chapter Eleven. Job Models are particularly critical if the new organization requires new jobs or jobs with new responsibilities. Only through Job Models will the specifics of the new structure be communicated to the people who will make it work.

Step 8: Structure the Human Performance System for Each Job. The failures of many reorganizations are not due to flawed organization charts. Reorganizations fail either because they suboptimize process performance (see Step 4) or because the new structure is not reinforced by the Human Performance Systems in which people work. The Human Performance System (described in depth in Chapter Six) includes the *capacity* of the people selected for jobs, their *skills and knowledge,* and the environment in which they work. A manager establishes an environment that supports the new structure by communicating *performance specifications* (the outputs and goals in the Job Model), removing current or potential *task interference* (barriers to doing the job), structuring *consequences* (rewards) that reinforce meeting the goals, and providing regular *feedback* on job performance.

Step 9: Establish Management Processes. Once the infrastructure for the new organization has been established at the Organization, Process, and Job/Performer Levels, the system has to be managed. The management process for implementing a new organization structure includes the actions that we introduced in the sections on management in Chapters Four, Five, and Six:

- Goal setting
- Performance management
- Resource allocation
- Interface ("white space") management
- Human Performance System management

Designing an Organization Structure That Works

Ace Copiers, Inc., is a real organization whose name and product have been somewhat modified for presentation here. To establish an organization structure that would work, Ace followed the nine-step process just described. An outline of that process follows, with selected artifacts.

Step 1: Establish a Clear Strategy. Ace Copiers, Inc., designs, manufactures, distributes, and services office photocopy machines and accessories. During an eighteen-month period, its previous trend of rapid growth slowed, and it lost a significant portion of its market share. Ace introduced only two new products in three years, which was far below the industry average. The development and production of both products went over budget, and neither copier sold well.

These problems motivated Ace's Management Committee to go through a period of soul searching. They went off to the mountains and

Figure 12.3. Ace Copiers, Inc., Original Organization Chart.

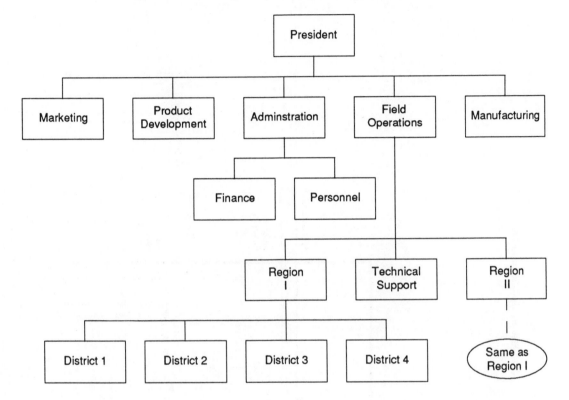

returned with a comprehensive strategy. An integral part of that strategy was to introduce two new products during each of the next five years.

Step 2: Document and Analyze the Current ("Is") Organization System. Figure 12.3 displays Ace's original organization chart. Figure 12.4 shows the original Relationship Map and its disconnects.

Step 3: Document and Analyze the Current ("Is") Processes. Given its strategy and the disconnects in its system, Ace identified product development and introduction as its most critical process. A cross-functional group developed an "is" Process Map and identified the disconnects.

Step 4: Develop "Should" Process Flows and Measures. Figure 12.5 displays a portion of the "should" map that the Ace team developed for product development and introduction. After completing the map, the team developed a set of measures for product development and introduction. Those measures led to a set of standards:

Figure 12.4. Ace Copiers, Inc., "Is" Relationship Map and Disconnects.

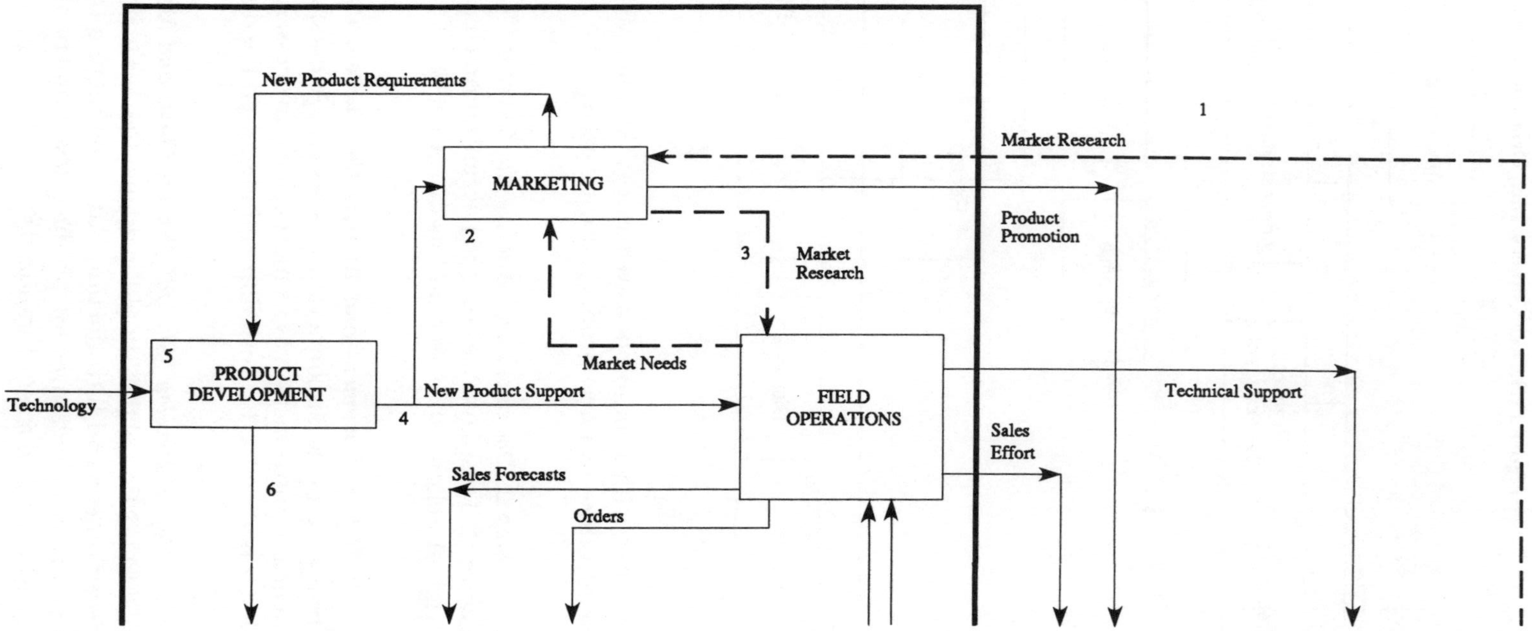

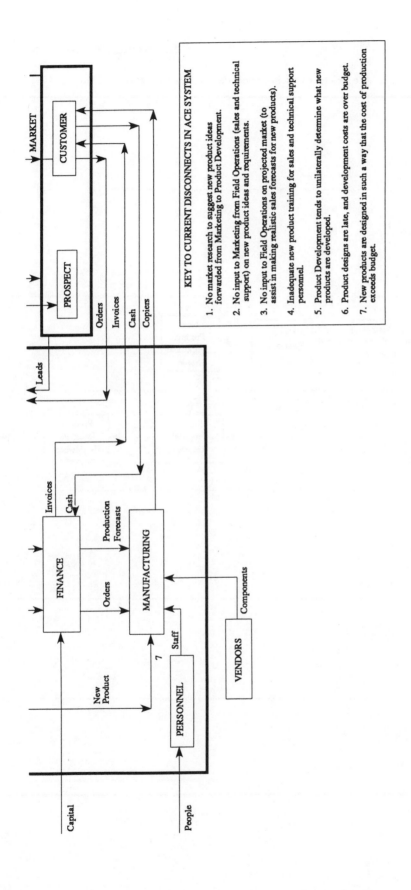

KEY TO CURRENT DISCONNECTS IN ACE SYSTEM

1. No market research to suggest new product ideas forwarded from Marketing to Product Development.

2. No input to Marketing from Field Operations (sales and technical support) on new product ideas and requirements.

3. No input to Field Operations on projected market (to assist in making realistic sales forecasts for new products).

4. Inadequate new product training for sales and technical support personnel.

5. Product Development tends to unilaterally determine what new products are developed.

6. Product designs are late, and development costs are over budget.

7. New products are designed in such a way that the cost of production exceeds budget.

Figure 12.5. Ace Product Development: Partial "Should" Process Map.

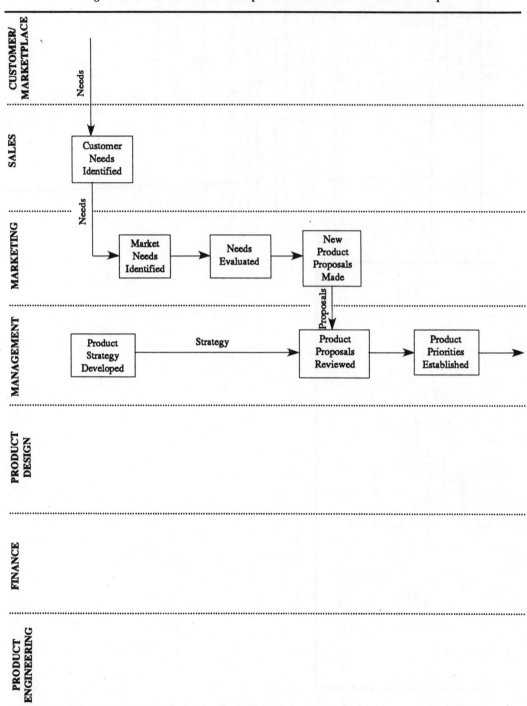

Figure 12.5. Ace Product Development: Partial "Should" Process Map, Cont'd.

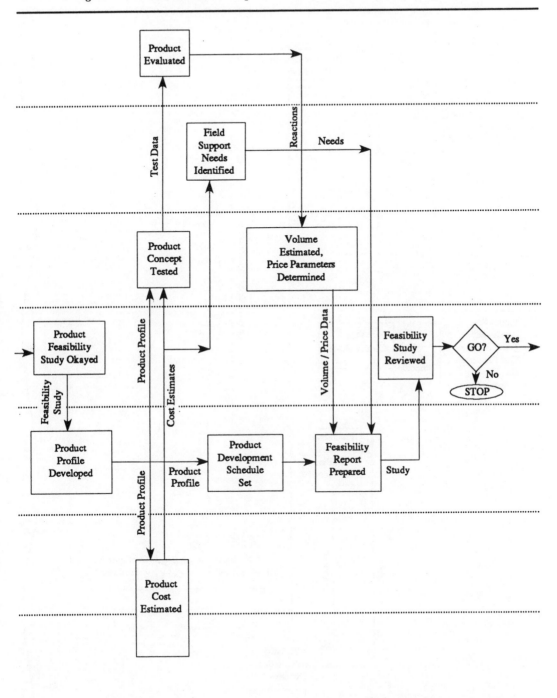

Figure 12.5. Ace Product Development: Partial "Should" Process Map, Cont'd.

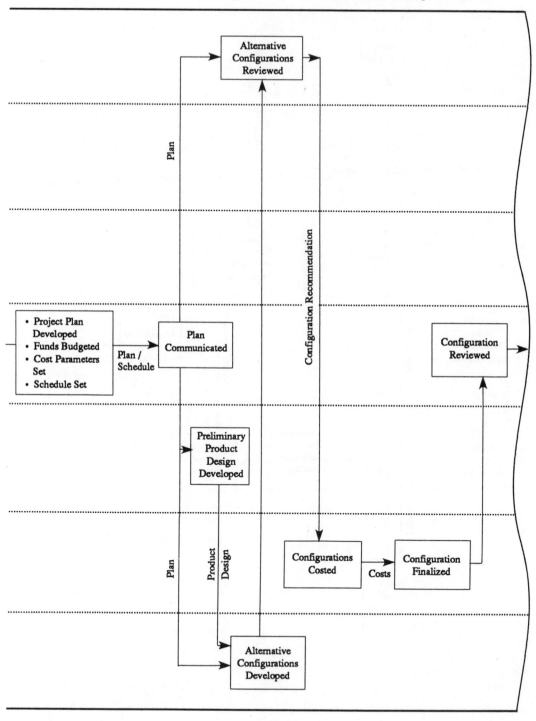

- New products will achieve sales volume and dollar goals.
- New products will be introduced (from conception to field training and production of the first five thousand units) within nine months.
- Unit cost of new products will be within established budget.
- Development and introduction costs will be within established budget.

These end-of-line measures and standards spawned submeasures and standards at critical junctures in the process.

Step 5: Design the Organization Chart. As the steps in the "should" product development process were being entered into the bands in the Process Map, the team members were assigning responsibilities to each function. They decided to split the old Product Development function into Product Design (which did the conceptualization) and Product Engineering (which was responsible for the internal and external configuration of the copier). The new Product Design function combined with Marketing and Sales to form an integrated Field Operations unit.

This Field Operations structure enabled Ace to make faster product development decisions and to speed up the implementation of those decisions. The establishment of the Product Engineering function in Manufacturing enabled Ace to configure copiers that could be made at a lower cost.

Before the organization chart was finalized, it was tested against other key Ace processes. Ace wanted to make sure it didn't establish a structure that optimized its product development process and suboptimized other critical processes. (If functional isolation can be illustrated by silos, perhaps process isolation can be seen as tunnels.) Figure 12.6 displays the new Ace organization chart. Figure 12.7 displays the new Relationship Map.

Step 6: Develop Function Models for Each Department. To make sure that the responsibilities of the new functions were clear, the Ace team developed a product development Role/Responsibility Matrix. A portion of this matrix appears in Table 12.1. Measures and goals were added to the process responsibilities assigned to each function. These responsibilities (outputs) and goals became each department's Function Model.

Step 7: Develop Job Models for Each Job. Task teams in each department used the Function Model as the basis for developing a Job Model for each job that contributed to the product development process (e.g., Sales Representative, Market Research Analyst, and Design Engineer). These Job Models contained the outputs that incumbents were expected to produce to contribute to the function outputs and the goals they were expected to achieve for each output.

Figure 12.6. New Ace Organization Chart.

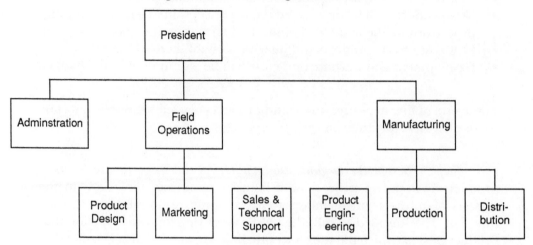

Step 8: Structure the Human Performance System for Each Job. For each job, the required feedback, rewards, and training were specified.

Step 9: Establish Management Processes. Once the new organization was established at the Organization, Process, and Job/Performer Levels, Ace installed an infrastructure for managing all Three Levels. The top management team created a series of management processes to ensure that goals were continuously set, performance was tracked against these goals at all Three Levels, resources were allocated so that the product development process was optimized, interfaces were managed, and all components of the Human Performance System were managed. These responsibilities became the core of the managers' performance appraisal.

Summary

Designing an organization structure is more than naming, arranging, and filling the boxes on the organization chart. While clear reporting relationships are administratively essential, getting products and services to customers requires an organization structure that focuses on the nature and flow of work. Toward this end, the first need is to decide what work is to be done (see Step 1). The next need is to understand how work currently gets accomplished (see Steps 2 and 3) and to design the way it should be carried out (see Step 4). Then and only then can a useful organization chart be created. In our opinion, form (structure) follows function (processes).

Our definition of organization structure encompasses the Organization Level of Performance (where strategy is set and customer-supplier relationships are established), the Process Level (where work flows are stream-

Figure 12.7. Ace "Should" Relationship Map.

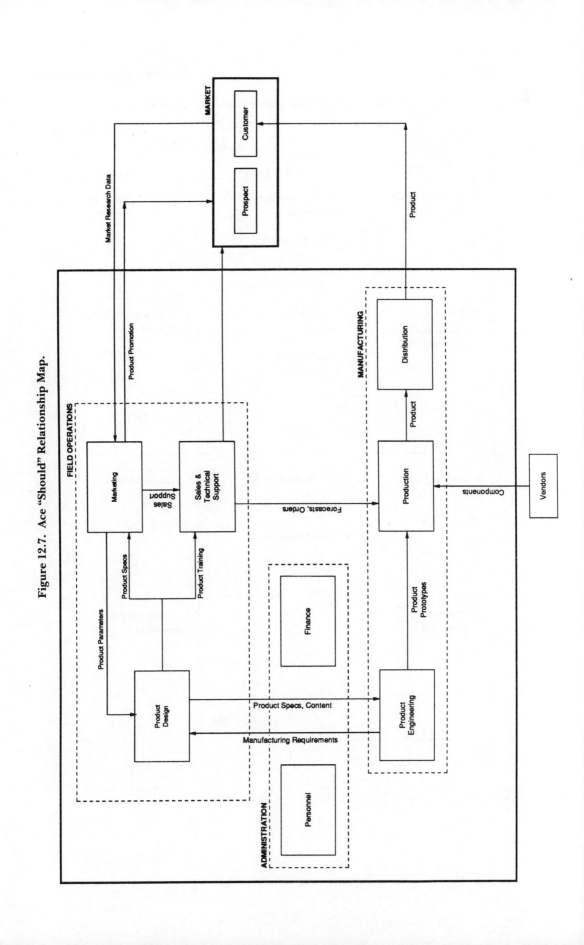

Table 12.1. Ace Product Development Role/Responsibility Summary.

New Product Development Process Steps	Functions and	
	Field Operations	
	Management	Sales
1. Product Needs Determined	• Product Strategy Developed • Product Additions Reviewed • Products Prioritized	• Customer Needs Identified
2. Product Feasibility Determined	• Feasibility Study Okayed • Feasibility Study Reviewed	• Field Support Needs Identified
3. Project Plan Developed	• Cost Parameters Set • Schedule Set • Funds Budgeted • Plan Communicated	• Plan Received
4. Product Designed		• Configurations Reviewed

Sales
Function Model

Table 12.1. Ace Product Development Role/Responsibility Summary, Cont'd.

Responsibilities		
Field Operations		**Manufacturing**
Marketing	**Product Design**	**Product Engineering**
• Market Needs Identified • Needs Evaluated • New Product Recommendation Made		
• Product Concept Tested • Volume Estimated • Price Parameters Determined	• Product Profile Developed • Product Development Schedule Set • Feasibility Report Prepared	• Product Cost Estimated
• Plan Received	• Plan Received	• Plan Received
	• Preliminary Product Design Developed	• Alternative Configurations Developed • Configurations Costed • Configurations Finalized
Marketing Function Model	Product Design Function Model	Product Engineering Function Model

lined and documented), and the Job/Performer Level (where jobs are defined and a supportive Human Performance System is installed). Critical dimensions of the structure at all Three Levels are performance measures and a management process through which the structure is continuously improved.

We are by no means saying that an organization structure that supports business processes is free of headaches. Managers may still have to contend with trade-offs between response time and cost, for example. However, with critical processes and Process Goals in the driver's seat, they can intelligently make and communicate those trade-offs.

Somewhere along the spectrum — between "maximum responsiveness at any cost" and "minimum cost, and we'll respond when we can" — lies the position desired by most organizations. Once that position has been determined (as part of strategy formulation), the processes (first) and the reporting relationships (second) can be designed to achieve it. To ensure that the position is attained and then maintained, managers can establish responsiveness and cost goals and can closely monitor performance against those goals.

The good news is that many of the variables that we have historically believed to be in conflict are not trade-offs at all. We have frequently found that a process designed for maximum quality is also a process designed for minimum cost.

,◆,▲▼▲▼▲▼▲▼▲▼▲▼▲▼▲▼▲▼▲▼▲▼▲▼▲▼▲▼▲▼▲▼▲▼▲▼▲▼◆,

CHAPTER 13

MANAGING ORGANIZATIONS AS SYSTEMS

Labor can do nothing without capital, capital nothing without labor, and neither labor nor capital can do anything without the guiding genius of management.

— *W. L. Mackenzie King*

You shouldn't expect most of your managers to exhibit "guiding genius." However, you should expect guiding competence. A competent manager understands the way his or her organization functions and is able to manage the variables that can make it better. Chapter Two is devoted to our world view, which includes the belief that organizations (at all levels) function as adaptive systems. Because your organization operates as a system, you will be most effective if you manage it as a system.

Building a System That Works

Before you begin managing your organization as a system, you should build a logical system to manage. We will illustrate the process with Computec, Inc., the organization we have used frequently as an example. Computec's top managers were concerned about the plateauing of the company's revenues and its loss of market share. They began to address the situation by building an intelligent system.

1. The top team formulated a strategy that addressed the current external (marketplace, competitive, and economic) reality. To develop this strategy, Computec management answered the questions presented in Chapter Seven. As part of that strategy, the top team decided to establish competitive advantages in three areas: the extent of Computec's customer service, the appeal of its continuous stream of innovative new products, and the speed with which it fills orders for its packaged software products.

2. The team developed an understanding of the current system by

creating a Computec Relationship Map (see Chapter Four). Team members realized that they would benefit by constructing and analyzing this picture of their business system themselves. As a result, they resisted the temptation to delegate this task to an analyst.

3. The top team overlaid the Organization Level (strategic) goals on the Map.

4. The team identified the eight Computec cross-functional processes and selected those that had (and still have) the greatest impact on the Organization Goals. On the basis of Computec's intended competitive advantages, the management team selected four strategically critical processes: product development and introduction (which, in Chapter Five, we called a *customer process*), order filling (another customer process), purchasing (an *administrative process*), and operational planning (a *management process*).

5. The team appointed a Vice President to serve as the Process Owner (see Chapter Ten) for each of the four processes.

6. As a team, top management developed the customer-driven, end-of-line Process Goals for each of the four strategic processes. The management team answered this question: Given our Organization Goals, what performance do we require from this process?

7. The group formed Process Teams, which documented and analyzed the four processes, using the Process Improvement steps described in Chapter Ten. The three key outputs of these teams were a recommended "should" process (which became the detailed roadmap for fixing the organization), a recommended plan for moving from "is" to "should," and a recommended set of goals for critical segments of the process.

8. The top team integrated the recommendations, so that all four processes could work in harmony. (The management team didn't want the product development process, for example, to be optimized at the expense of the other processes.)

9. The team implemented the "should" processes, which included changing process flows, changing the assignment of functional responsibilities (and, in some instances, the organization structure), establishing a Performance Measurement/Management System around the Process Goals and the functional goals that they spawned (see Chapter Eleven), and changing job responsibilities and Human Performance Systems as necessary (see Chapter Six). Since changing all four processes at once was more than Computec could handle, the top team phased the implementation.

Evaluating the System

The changes have been successfully implemented. Computec has built a system that works. Now the top team's challenge is to manage the system it has built. However, before the system can be effectively managed, it is necessary to develop a mechanism for measuring and evaluating key components of the system. Toward this end, Computec developed the following:

• A report card for evaluating the performance of each of the four strategic processes. Areas for evaluation include customer feedback, internal requirements (such as performance against budget), ability to respond to change, and extent of continuous improvement. The data for the evaluation come directly from the performance measurement system, which documents actual performance and compares it to the Process Goals (see Step 9).

• A report card for evaluating each Process Owner in terms of his or her contribution to the effectiveness of the process. The items on this report card are based on top management's clear delineation of the responsibilities of the Process Owner (see the sample list in Chapter Ten). For example, Computec Process Owners are evaluated on how well they keep the rest of the top team informed of process performance and how well they help resolve any "white space" conflicts between functions.

• A report card for evaluating the Vice President of each function on how well that function supports the processes to which it contributes. For example, the Vice President of Marketing is evaluated on how well Marketing supports product development and introduction. The evaluation is based on the process steps carried out by that function and on the functional goals (in such areas as customer requirements and budget) that evolved from the Process Goals. The Computec Function Models (see Chapter Eleven) were particularly useful in the development of these rating categories.

Vice Presidents are evaluated not only on how well their functions achieve their goals but also in "softer" areas, such as degree of cooperation with other functions for the good of the process, responsiveness to changes required for process success, and the degree to which Human Performance Systems support individuals and teams who contribute to process success. The performance appraisals of the four Process Owners assess them both as Process Owners and as leaders of functions that exist to support processes.

The Systems Management Processes

At this point, Computec has created a system that makes sense, and the company has developed mechanisms for evaluating the key aspects of that system: the processes, the Process Owners, and the function managers. Now let's examine the ways in which some of the basic management processes help the senior management team manage Computec as a system.

In the *annual planning process*, the Computec President, Process Owners, and Vice Presidents:

• Update the strategy and operating plan.
• Identify new Organization Level outputs and Organization Goals.

- Confirm the identity of the strategic processes and update Process Goals to ensure that they reflect Organization Goals.
- Identify the process changes required to meet the new Process Goals. These changes may include modifications to the processes themselves, new goals for process segments, or resource shifts.

In the *annual budgeting process*, the same players:

- Negotiate budgets for the processes, which are based on the Process Goals that were established as part of the planning process. (The Process Owners' commitment to budget allocation is particularly critical.)
- Negotiate function budgets, which are based on the process budgets and on each function's contributions to the Process Goals.
- Roll up the process and function budgets and marry them with the organizationwide budget, which was established in the strategy.

In the *monthly operations-review process*, the top managers:

- Examine product and market performance in terms of customer satisfaction goals.
- Examine product and market performance in terms of revenue and profit goals.
- Examine cost performance in terms of budget goals.
- Examine process performance in terms of the Process Goals established for customer satisfaction, revenue and profit, and cost. Each function's performance is reviewed in terms of the degree to which it is providing the agreed-upon process support. At this step in the review, the team is ready to ask a number of questions:

  - Why is performance better (or worse) than we expected? Is this a blip or a trend? Is this a surprise? If so, why? Is the process flawed? Did functional priorities supersede process priorities? Is our goal setting, planning, or budgeting deficient?
  - Do we need to add to or modify our goals?
  - Do we need to reallocate resources? If so, which process or function gets more? How much more, and from where?

During the operations-review meeting, the President asks the questions. The Process Owners provide most of the answers and are supported by the function heads. The answers lead to decisions, which in turn result in action items that are assigned to individuals. These action items are documented and categorized as changes in policy, changes in goals, changes in resources, changes in processes, changes in reporting relationships, and changes in management practices.

In the *biannual performance review process*, the President provides grades for the processes, Process Owners, and function managers. These ratings serve as the basis for the annual allocation of bonus money. The size of the bonus pot is determined by the profitability of the company. We believe that this scenario has some key distinctions from traditional management:

- Because the measures are customer-focused, the customer's voice is heard throughout the performance review process.
- Because the goals are process-driven, the top team is able to review the performance of the business comprehensively.
- Because the goals are process-driven, the top team can review both the results and the ways in which those results are achieved. Since the team understands the reasons for the results, it has greater control over the business.
- Because the Process Owner plays a key role in the management process, the voices of "the way work gets done" and of "white-space management" are never drowned out by other considerations.
- Because functional goals are subordinate to process goals, no departmental head can command an inappropriate share of the resources.
- Because all Three Levels are incorporated into the Performance Management process, change is more intelligently managed. The top team is less likely to make strategy or policy decisions without developing an implementation plan that includes actions at the Process and Job/Performer Levels; to initiate systems improvements without determining their impact on the Organization and Job/Performer Levels; or to take action to improve employees' performance, other than in response to the needs of the Organization and Process Levels.

The Systems Management Culture

We have found that the culture of an organization in which systems are being managed differs from the culture of a typical organization. Table 13.1 contrasts the traditional (vertical) and systems (horizontal) cultures. Within a systems culture, we find that managers at all levels are able to answer yes to the systems management questions contained in Table 13.2.

Summary

Managing organizations as systems involves understanding and managing the nine Performance Variables that serve as the theme of this book. The business system is made up of inputs, outputs, and feedback at the Organization, Process, and Job/Performer Levels. At each of the Three Levels, the system requires clear and appropriate goals, logical design, and supportive management practices.

Table 13.1. Comparison of the Traditional (Vertical) and Systems (Horizontal) Cultures.

Traditional Culture	Systems Culture
• Functional needs dominate decision making.	• Customer and process needs dominate decision making.
• Functions have minimal interaction with other functions.	• Functions have extensive interaction with other functions.
• Most people understand only the functions in which they work.	• People understand the big picture and the business of the other functions with which they need to collaborate.
• People do not know the identity of and linkages with their functions' internal customers and suppliers.	• People understand the inputs and outputs that link their functions to other functions.
• Interactions among functions tend to be confrontational.	• Interactions among functions tend to focus on "win-win" problem solving and decision making.
• Functions are competitors.	• Functions are collaborative partners.
• A function's measures isolate it from other functions.	• A function's measures reflect the contribution it should make to its immediate customer and to the system as a whole.
• A function can look good at the expense of other functions.	• A function can look good only through its contribution to the entire organization.
• Only results are measured and managed.	• Results and processes are measured and managed.
• Systems are examined only when there is a problem ("If it ain't broke, don't fix it").	• Systems are continually analyzed and improved ("We're not as good as we could be").
• Information is not regularly shared among functions.	• Information of mutual interest is routinely shared among functions.
• Managers do not allow employees to resolve issues directly with peers in other functions; they expect them to raise issues through the chain of command.	• Managers encourage employees to resolve issues with peers in other functions.
• Employees' involvement in decision making is nonexistent or confined to the function.	• Cross-functional teams at all levels are convened frequently to address critical business issues.
• Employees are rewarded for their functional contributions.	• Employees are rewarded for their organizational contributions.

Performance measures provide the latticework of the system. A Three Levels measurement system provides a window on more than just results. By monitoring and improving those factors that influence results, managers are able to cause more systemic improvement and to understand what's needed to implement change.

Managers become heroes in the systems management culture by understanding their business, collaborating with other departments to get a job done, subordinating the optimization of their departments to the common good of the process, and creating Human Performance Systems that equip people to make their maximum contributions to the system and that reinforce them when they do.

Table 13.2. Systems Management Questions.

- Does your department have a strategy that is linked to the organizationwide strategy?
- Can you identify all of your department's internal and external customers?
- Do you know all of your department's products and services?
- Do you know your customers' requirements for your department's products and services?
- Do you measure performance on the basis of how well your products and services meet your customers' requirements?
- Can you identify your department's internal and external suppliers?
- Do you establish clear goals for the products and services provided to your department by your suppliers?
- Do you have documentation of your department's role in the cross-functional processes to which it contributes?
- Do you measure your department on the degree to which it contributes to cross-functional processes?
- Do you measure the "upstream" performance of the processes that flow through your department?
- Do you have tracking and feedback systems that effectively and efficiently gather performance information and provide it to the people who need it?
- Do you have the skills to troubleshoot (remove the root causes of) performance gaps in your system?
- Do you spend a large percentage of your time working to improve the interfaces ("white space") between your department and other departments and between subunits within your department?
- Do employees in your department work in an environment where their job design, goals, feedback, rewards, resources, and training enable them to make their maximum contributions to process efficiency and effectiveness?

‹‹

CHAPTER 14

CREATING A PERFORMANCE-BASED HUMAN RESOURCE DEVELOPMENT FUNCTION

Genius will live and thrive without training.
                                                    —Margaret Fuller

In most organizations, training is a sizable investment, more sizable than senior managers realize. They know the amount of the Human Resource Development Department's budget. However, the total investment in training, which includes salaries of participants, is less visible and would be a surprise to most executives. Of more significance is the fact that even fewer of them know the return they are getting on that investment. Can you envision a manager who *could not* cite the return on his investment in a $50,000 telecommunications system? Can you envision a manager who *could* tell you the return he is getting on a $50,000 investment in communications training for managers?

Training is often seen as an employee benefit (like company picnics or contributions to the insurance plan), which is not expected to provide a tangible return. Isn't training just part of enlightened management, intrinsically good and unquestionably valuable in unmeasurable ways?

No. Training should be treated like other investments.

- If the return on a given training investment is not easily quantified, how can a manager describe the specific benefits to the organization of that training effort?
- How is the investment in training to be assessed (and compared to other potential investments) *before* the investment is made?
- If top managers are committed to spending a certain percentage of revenue on training, how can they be sure that they are investing in the *right* training?

The answer to all three of these questions is the same. With the exception of situations in which an employee is being developed for a new

Figure 14.1. The "Vacuum" View of Performance.

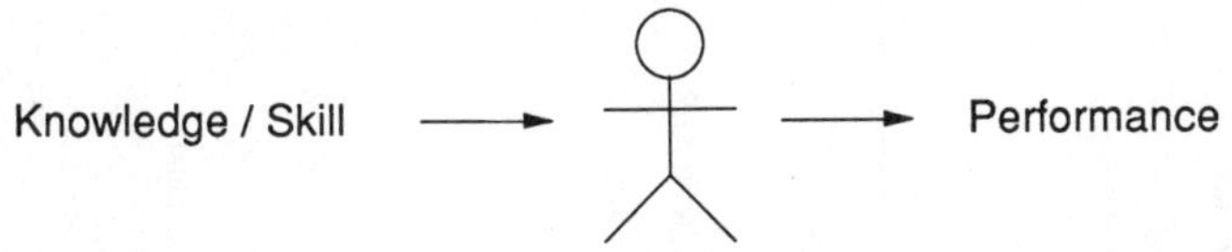

Knowledge / Skill ⟶ Performance

job, the purpose of training is to improve current performance. Therefore, training should be assessed in terms of its impact on performance.

Two Views of Performance Improvement

There are two views of performance. In the prevailing view, people exist in a vacuum. If managers want to establish or improve a certain performance *output*, all they need to do is arrange for the proper training *input*. Figure 14.1 shows this limited perspective. When people in the Human Resource Development Department hold this view, their response to a request for training tends to be "You got it. When do you want it? Do you have enough money for a videotape?"

Unfortunately, the world of performance is not simply "skills and knowledge in/performance out." This reality leads to the second view of performance: the systems view. In the systems view, represented by the Nine Variables that serve as the theme of this book, human performance is a function of:

- *The Job/Performer Level*, where job outputs are defined and the Human Performance System establishes the environment in which people work
- *The Process Level*, where business processes establish the work flows in which people work
- *The Organization Level*, where the strategy provides the direction and the organization configuration provides the structure in which people work

Every trainee (or potential trainee) is a *performer* who functions within all Three Levels of Performance and is influenced by each of the nine Performance Variables. As Table 14.1 shows, Skills and Knowledge (which is all training can provide) is one small part of one of the nine Performance Variables. Without the perspective of the Three Levels, training is likely to be prescribed when training is not needed. When not supported by the Human Performance System, by work processes, and strategy and structure, training which is needed is nevertheless sure to fail.

The systems (Three Levels) view has significant implications for the Human Resources Development (HRD) function, particularly because training is one of management's favorite performance improvement solutions.

Table 14.1. Training's Role in the Nine Performance Variables.

Performance Needs

Performance Levels	GOALS	DESIGN	MANAGEMENT
ORGANIZATION LEVEL	ORGANIZATION GOALS • Has the organization's strategy/direction been articulated and communicated? • Does this strategy make sense, in terms of the external threats and opportunities and the internal strengths and weaknesses? • Given this strategy, have the required outputs of the organization and the level of performance expected from each output been determined and communicated?	ORGANIZATION DESIGN • Are all relevant functions in place? • Are there unnecessary functions? • Is the current flow of inputs and outputs between functions appropriate? • Does the formal organization structure support the strategy and enhance the efficiency of the system?	ORGANIZATION MANAGEMENT • Have appropriate function goals been set? • Is relevant performance measured? • Are resources appropriately allocated? • Are the interfaces between functions being managed?
PROCESS LEVEL	PROCESS GOALS • Are goals for key processes linked to customer/organization requirements?	PROCESS DESIGN • Is this the most efficient/effective process for accomplishing the Process Goals?	PROCESS MANAGEMENT • Have appropriate process sub-goals been set? • Is process performance managed? • Are sufficient resources allocated to each process? • Are the interfaces between process steps being managed?
JOB / PERFORMER LEVEL	JOB / PERFORMER GOALS • Are job outputs and standards linked to process requirements (which are in turn linked to customer and organization requirements?)	JOB DESIGN • Are process requirements reflected in the appropriate jobs? • Are job steps in a logical sequence? • Have supportive policies and procedures been developed? • Is the job environment ergonomically sound?	JOB / PERFORMER MANAGEMENT • Do the performers understand the Job Goals (outputs they are expected to produce and the standards they are expected to meet)? • Do the performers have sufficient resources, clear signals and priorities, and a logical job design? • Are the performers rewarded for achieving the Job Goals? • Do the performers know if they are meeting the Job Goals? • Do the performers have the necessary knowledge/skill to achieve the Job Goals? • If the performers were in an environment in which the five questions listed above were answered "yes," would they have the physical, mental, and emotional capacity to achieve the Job Goals?

HRD is often asked to bring about major organizational change with the small lever shown in Table 14.2. A review of the Nine Variables framework shows that job performance is a function of Job Performance Goals, Job Design, and Job/Performance Management, where Skills and Knowledge is but *one* of six factors. In twenty-six years of experience, we have seldom seen a job performance "problem" that could be significantly improved by manipulating the Skills and Knowledge (Training) factor alone. *Senior management should either provide HRD with a longer lever or realize that HRD's influence on organization performance is important but very limited.*

The Three Levels context and tools have implications for all areas of HRD. We will devote the rest of this chapter to exploring four of these areas:

- Determining training and development needs
- Designing training
- Evaluating training
- Designing and managing the HRD function

Determining Training and Development Needs

Our basic assumption is that HRD is in the performance improvement business. The question that should be asked in planning and implementing all HRD interventions is how this activity affects the performance of the business.

HRD can discover training needs in two ways: reactively (in response to requests for training) and proactively (as a result of planning to meet organization needs through training). The Three Levels approach can help identify training needs in both situations.

Reacting to Requests for Training. When responding to a request for training, the HRD professional must realize that the requester probably has not conducted a thorough analysis and most likely does not know the limitations of training as a performance improvement intervention. All he or she knows is that there is a feeling of pain. The HRD Needs Analyst's primary objective has to be to understand the performance context of the request. Only through that understanding can he or she determine whether any training is needed and, if so, the specific objectives that the training should meet.

As section A of Figure 14.2 shows, the ideal response to a request for training follows an "outside-in" process. It begins at the Organization Level and moves through the Process Level to the Job Level. Sometimes political factors prevent the HRD analyst from beginning at the Organization Level. Under these circumstances, we recommend the less ideal (but still performance-based) "inside-out" process displayed in the B section of Figure 14.2.

The ideal needs-analysis process is more likely to get at the real issues

Figure 14.2. Two Approaches to Training-Needs Analysis.

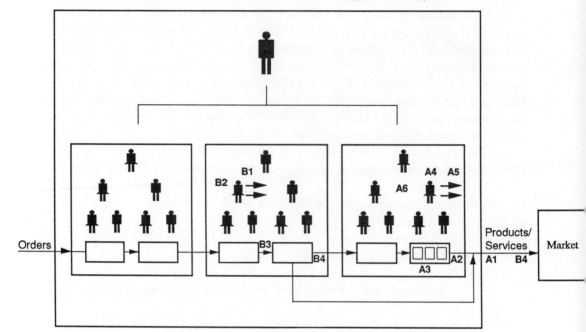

behind the training request and is more likely to unearth performance needs that cannot be met by training. However, it may be more risky because it goes beyond what is normally expected of the HRD function. It also tends to be more time-consuming. The "sometimes necessary" approach, while less countercultural and time-intensive, may not address the most significant organization need. While the analyst does verify the need for training before proceeding with any development, he or she is locked into the assumption that the person identified by the requester represents the greatest performance improvement opportunity.

To illustrate the ideal process, let us examine a request for training. Sharon Pfeiffer, the Vice President for Operations at Property Casualty, Inc. (PCI), the partially fictionalized company introduced in Chapter Nine, has asked Stephen Willaby, the Director of HRD, for a comprehensive training program for incumbent Claim Representatives. She tells him that Claim Reps' training is a high priority for her this fiscal year and that she will provide the funding from the Operations budget.

If Stephen sees the Vice President's request as a trigger to conduct a training-needs analysis he will most likely use one of these three techniques:

- A training-needs survey, in which Reps and their managers are asked to identify the skills and knowledge required to perform the Claim Rep job
- A competency study, in which a group of Reps and Claim managers are

asked to identify the general competencies of an effective Claim Rep (analysis, computation, and written and oral communication)
- A task analysis, in which effective Claim Reps provide a list of the tasks they perform while doing their job

Any of these three approaches is better than developing a program without a needs analysis. They gather some real-world information, they can be done quickly and inexpensively, and they are not risky for Stephen. However, these methodologies share a significant weakness: none of them is tied directly to the organization, process, and job *outputs* that are the reason the Claim Representative job exists. Knowledge and skills, competencies, and tasks are all *inputs* to the results that PCI expects the Reps to produce.

The failure of these three techniques to focus on performance outputs would be misguided if Stephen were being asked to develop entry-level training for Claim Reps. In this situation, however, his input focus is worse than misguided. At best, it is wasteful; at worst, it is dangerous. Because the Vice President has requested the course for *incumbent* Reps, we can assume that she wants to improve current performance. The course or curriculum that results from any of these three needs-analysis techniques *may* address the true performance needs that spawned the request; but is this training buried in a sea of material that covers parts of the Claim Rep job that are being performed satisfactorily? Is training *of any kind* for Claim Reps the solution to Sharon's concern? Is the Claim Rep job the one that should be addressed? *What's the real performance need?* If Stephen were to take the ideal approach outlined in section A of Figure 14.2, he would:

1. Identify, at the Organization Level, the Critical Business Issue — the performance problem or opportunity of concern to the Vice President. Are there too many errors in processed claims, causing complaints from claimants and extensive rework? Are the payout amounts to claimants too high? Does Sharon see an opportunity for PCI to establish a competitive advantage in the area of claim processing time?

2. Identify, at the Process Level, the business process that has the greatest impact on the Critical Business Issue. Let's say that it's the claim adjudication process.

3. Use a Process Map (see Chapter Five) to document the adjudication process and to identify any gaps between desired and actual performance of each process step.

4. Identify the job(s) that have an impact on the performance of the process steps in which there are gaps. Perhaps those jobs are Claim Rep and Claim Supervisor.

5. Develop a list of the desired outputs of Reps and Supervisors. Identify which of the desired outputs are not being produced.

6. Identify the causes of any subpar outputs. Possible causes (covered in depth in Chapter Six) include missing or inadequate Performance Specifi-

cations; Task Interference; missing or unaligned Consequences; missing or inadequate Feedback; lack of Skills or Knowledge; and lack of Individual Capacity.

Stephen would develop training only for the Skills and Knowledge needs. Ideally, he would have the charter to recommend changes in nontraining (environmental) areas as well.

During this six-step process (a distillation of the fourteen-step performance improvement process described in Chapter Nine), Stephen would most likely visit the claims office that is performing best (in terms of measures related to the Critical Business Issue) and two or three other offices. In each office, the required information could be gathered by interviewing the Office Manager and by interviewing and observing effective and ineffective Claim Supervisors and Reps.

The PCI request was actually made by an insurance company executive. Fortunately, the real Stephen arranged for a Three Levels analysis. As it turned out, the job that was having the most impact on the Critical Business Issue (excessive claim payouts) was Claim Supervisor. Thus, not only did Claim Reps not need training, *they were not even the performers with the greatest opportunity for improvement.* Claim Supervisors needed improvement in two of their job outputs: qualifying claims, and assigning claims to Claim Reps. Training was part of the solution, but the primary need was for a system of measurement and feedback. If the Director of HRD had responded unquestioningly to the request of the Vice President for Operations, he would have developed an impressive training program for Claim Reps—an impressive waste of PCI's money.

Proactively Planning for Human Resource Development. HRD professionals certainly should not try to do away with training requests. However, they should not be driven by training requests. The way out of the purely reactive mode is to initiate HRD plans. The steps in an HRD planning process are:

1. Identify major clients (by business unit or department, with a senior manager as the contact in each client organization).
2. Develop an HRD plan with the client contact. Begin by identifying the client organization's anticipated operating needs for the next eighteen months. These needs should be based on the business unit's strategy or the department's contribution to the strategy. On the basis of these needs, identify the training that will be required to meet them. The plan should outline what both the client and the HRD function are going to do to meet the plan.
3. Consolidate all of the business-unit HRD plans into a plan for the HRD function.
4. Review progress toward the plan with the client every six months.

5. Review progress at the end of the year and update the plan for the next year.

If an unplanned training request comes into the HRD function, an HRD representative and the client contact should discuss whether it represents an addition to or a replacement for something in the plan. If it is an addition, required resources can be negotiated with the client.

Even if HRD is limited to training interventions, this simple planning process results in clear priorities, which are based on the customer's long-term needs. It places the needs in the overall performance context of the business, and it enables the HRD department to make its resource decisions on a firmer business footing.

Designing Training

The "vacuum" view of performance leads to subject matter–driven training and development. Training programs tend to address the hot topic of the day, or perceptions of what "they" need.

Here is a typical example of a subject matter–driven training design. An HRD department was asked to train a large group of new people, whose job was to interview applicants for unemployment compensation. The design assignment was given to Matthew, a training specialist. He began by identifying subject matter areas relevant to the new interviewer. He examined existing bodies of knowledge concerning interviewing techniques and psychology. Matthew identified interviewing-technique subject matter areas, such as developing the types of questions to ask, using questioning and probing skills, and interpreting answers. While exploring interviewing psychology, he uncovered subject matter areas that focused on an interviewee's behavioral and personality makeup. After a considerable amount of apparently relevant subject matter research, Matthew developed a three-day course that made extensive use of videotape and role-play exercises.

The Three Levels view, by contrast, leads to performance-driven training and development based on the needs-analysis approach already described. Performance-driven training design (which fits well with the techniques described by others as Criterion-Referenced Instruction or Learner-Controlled Instruction) suggests the approach used in the following example. Gwen, the educational technologist who was given the new-hire interviewing-training assignment, began by determining what the new interviewer was expected to do on the job. Specifically, she identified all of the decisions that the interviewer was expected to make, particularly the final decision (output) of the typical interview. From this analysis, Gwen learned that in all cases the interviewer's output was to decide where to refer the interviewees. There were four possibilities: Office A, where the applicants would receive unemployment compensation; Office B, where the applicants would be referred to jobs (because they were able to work and didn't qualify for compensation); Office C, where the applicants were interviewed by a psychiatrist (because they had psychological problems that would interfere with job placement); and Office D, where they were interviewed by the Chief Interviewer (because the applicants presented special problems or didn't clearly belong in one of the other three offices). On the basis of this information, Gwen concluded that the task of the new interviewers was primarily one of categorizing, or sorting. They were expected to decide which of the four offices to send applicants to. Thus, she decided that the subject matter of the training should consist of the following steps, presented in this sequence:

1. The four alternatives for the final decision
2. The criteria for each alternative (the conditions under which an applicant should be sent to each office)
3. The information required to make the final decision, on the basis of the criteria
4. Techniques for asking questions to elicit the required information

The resulting one-day course did not require elaborate instructional design or expensive media. It concentrated on teaching the interviewers to discriminate among the offices to which various applicants could be sent.

Without going through an exhaustive or overly formal analysis, Gwen addressed all Three Levels: she determined what the *organization* needed from the interviewer, she examined the interviewing *process*, and, on the basis of this information, she identified the skills and knowledge needed by the *performers*. Unlike Matthew, who based his course on an academic and generic model of interviewing skills, Gwen let the subject matter of the course be driven by the real world of her organization. Gwen's design was based on *performance*.

Evaluating Training

Evaluating training in a vacuum is a waste of time. A training program may have well-stated learning outcomes, appropriate media, excellent materials, and effective instruction. However, if the training addresses the wrong performance area, is not reinforced by Consequences and Feedback, is not supported by a well-designed work process, or is not linked to the direction of the organization, it is not worth the investment. With typical methods of evaluation, a workshop could win awards for instructional design the same week that the company files for Chapter 11 protection. Performance impact evaluation, by contrast, does not allow a course to look good without its also having a significant impact on the performance of the business.

Figure 14.3 shows where four types of evaluation fit in our basic systems diagram. All four types of evaluation are valid. The ideal course is

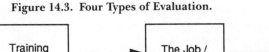

Figure 14.3. Four Types of Evaluation.

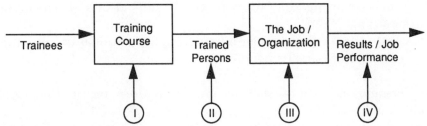

Type I.   Are the trainees happy with the course?
Type II.   Does the training course teach the concepts?
Type III. Are the concepts used on the job?
Type IV.   Does the application of the concepts positively affect the organization?

liked by trainees, teaches what needs to be taught, provides skills that are used on the job, and provides skills that have a positive impact on the performance of the organization. However, most evaluations are of Types I or II, which are "upstream" from the performance that ultimately matters. Performance impact evaluation focuses on Types III and IV.

One use of performance impact evaluation is to help avoid or eliminate unneeded training. For example, if the Director of Engineering has requested a workshop in report writing, it would be readily apparent how to evaluate trainees' satisfaction (a reaction questionnaire) and learning (a test). If, however, the requester would be unable to determine whether the new writing skills were being applied on the job and, more important, whether their application was having any effect on the Engineering Department's performance, the training would be a questionable investment.

Another use of performance impact evaluation is to identify areas in which management needs to support the training. For example, a training course on quality control would be fairly simple to assess with Type I and Type II evaluations. As Types III and IV are discussed, the HRD specialist and the client may realize that if management does not take action to support the use of the quality-control techniques (by providing resources and rewards), the best training in the world will have no effect on performance.

If the HRD analyst has determined the training needs, as just described, evaluation (especially Type IV) should not present a problem. Because the training needs directly affect documented organization performance problems or opportunities, the training can be evaluated in terms of its impact on those problems or opportunities. The questions that appear in column A of Figure 14.2 provide the framework for performance impact evaluation.

Designing and Managing the HRD Function

The Three Levels approach to determining training needs, to designing training, and to evaluating training suggests a different kind of HRD department. As a matter of fact, this type of HRD function can transform itself from a training operation to the organization's "Performance Department."

A Performance Department differs from a traditional training function in a number of ways. Its people:

- Understand that their mission is to improve performance, not to provide skills and knowledge.
- Only conduct training and development that are linked to organization performance needs.
- Only conduct training and development that are supported by the environment in which the trainees work (the Human Performance System).
- Evaluate training and development according to its contributions to organization performance needs.
- Conduct diagnoses that go beyond training- and development-needs analysis. They are interested and skilled in unearthing nontraining problems, such as Task Interference, poor Feedback, and unsupportive Consequences.
- Recommend solutions to both training and development and nontraining and development needs.
- Understand the business at all Three Levels and the influence of all nine Performance Variables.
- Understand that the department is a business and must be run as a business.

To expand upon the last bullet, the Performance Department is an organizational subsystem, it is subject to the systems laws described in Chapter Two. As a business, it also has a clear strategy (including a specific identification of products or services and customers), which is linked to the organizationwide strategy, and it is structured to run as a performance business whose subfunctions carry out needs analysis, design, development, delivery, and evaluation. Figure 14.4 shows one configuration for a Performance Department.

You should not infer from Figure 14.4 that a Performance Department must include a minimum of twenty people; a number of functions can be performed by the same person. As a matter of fact, the department in Figure 14.4 could be staffed by as few as three people.

Moving from the Organization Level to the Process Level, we see that the Performance Department includes the traditional training processes: course development, course delivery, and course evaluation. However, it also includes processes for organization, process, and job-needs analysis and for nontraining interventions (designing measurement systems, feedback systems, and consequence systems).

At the Job/Performer Level, the Performance Department structures jobs to include analysis, design, planning, evaluation, and consulting, as well as development and delivery responsibilities. Lastly, the manager of the Performance Department creates a Human Performance System that supports a holistic performance mission. Since the manager wants the Performance Department's staff to identify performance improvement opportunities and design multifaceted solutions, he or she *doesn't* measure the staff on "number of classroom days."

Frankly, we don't care whether it is the HRD department that assumes the role of Performance Department, as long as somebody does. We focus on HRD because that tends to be the natural place for this expertise and set of services to reside. However, we have worked with organizations where HRD fulfilled the traditional training role, and comprehensive performance diagnosis and improvement were the mission of a separate department.

Summary

We believe that HRD functions are uniquely positioned to become their organizations' Performance Departments (or, at least, performance-based HRD departments). Reflecting the Three Levels–based systems view, rather than the limited and potentially counterproductive "vacuum" view, Performance Departments realize that training is a very small lever with which to move the world, no matter where the fulcrum is placed. Their people identify needs and evaluate contributions at all Three Levels of Performance. They are as comfortable at the Organization and Process Levels and in nonperformer components of the Human Performance System as they are in the classroom, and they are incredible businesspeople who are making a demonstrably significant contribution to the company's competitive advantage.

Figure 14.4. Model of a Performance Focused Training Function.

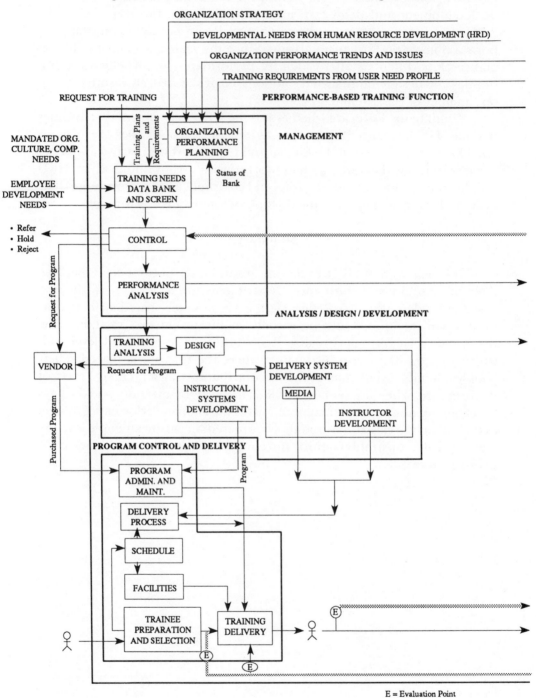

E = Evaluation Point

Figure 14.4. Model of a Performance Focused Training Function, Cont'd.

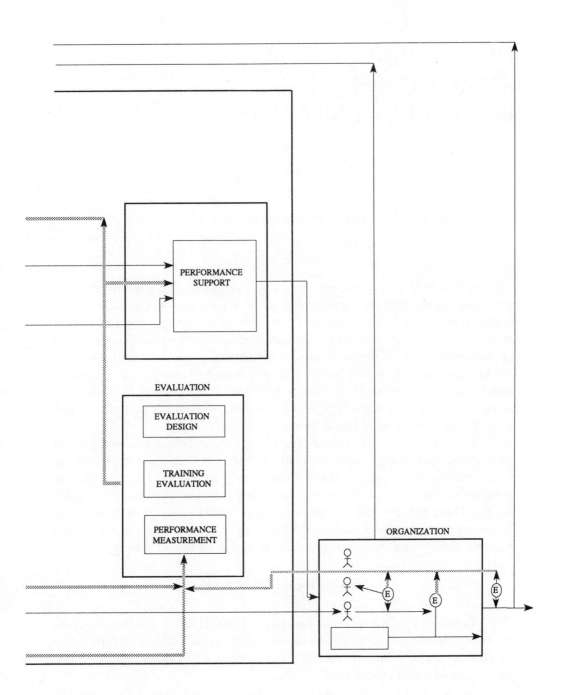

.ₐₐₐₐₐₐₐₐₐₐₐₐₐₐₐₐₐₐₐₐₐₐₐₐₐₐₐₐ.

DEVELOPING
AN ACTION PLAN
FOR IMPLEMENTATION

A journey of a thousand miles must begin with a single step.
— Lao Tzu

Say you believe that the systems view of an organization represents the way work gets done. You are determined to manage each component of the system you manage. You agree that the tools at all Three Levels of Performance should be at the heart of any comprehensive effort to formulate and implement strategy, improve quality, productivity, cycle time, and cost, and design an organization that works. You have vowed to use the questions that support each of the nine Performance Variables as the basis of your management system. However, you may feel a bit overwhelmed. At this point, your primary question is most likely "Where do I start?"

One way to start is by initiating a Three Levels project. Before there can be any widespread commitment to the Three Levels as a way of life in an organization, the approach must demonstrate its worth. The best way to make a short-term contribution and to show long-term potential is by applying the Three Levels tools to a strategic issue facing your organization. The following steps represent an initial Three Levels effort. They are stated in a way that should enable you to use them as the basis for an action plan.

Step 1: Organization Level

Convene a high-level cross-functional team. Develop a systems picture of your entire organization, or of a key segment within your organization. Use this picture to help identify an issue that is critical to the successful implementation of your organization's strategy.

We recommend that you use the Relationship Map format for the systems picture; guidelines and examples appear in Chapter Four. The issue will emerge from an examination of the Map in the light of the organization's key strategic goals. It may involve a current or potential competitive gap in quality, cycle time, or cost, or it may focus on the need to establish or enhance a competitive advantage through the introduction of a new product, service, or system.

Although you should certainly start with an opportunity with which you are comfortable, we suggest that you resist the temptation to pick an easy or minor issue just to see whether the approach works. The Three Levels tools can address an issue of any complexity; as a matter of fact, they are most helpful when an issue is multifaceted. The approach will prove its worth only if it is applied to an issue of significance.

Step 2: Process Level

Identify the cross-functional business process or processes that have the greatest impact on the issue highlighted in Step 1. Form a cross-functional Process Team to address the issue.

We recommend that you follow the Process Improvement project steps described in Chapter Ten. The eleven steps can be used as the substeps in your action plan. During this Process Improvement effort, the team should use Process Mapping to identify the changes needed to enhance the performance of the strategically critical process.

Step 3: Job/Performer Level

Identify one or more jobs critical to the successful implementation of the process improvements designed during Step 2. For each job, have the Process Team (along with job incumbents and supervisors) describe the outputs and goals required by the new process. Then ask the team to identify the environmental support that must be provided to the people in these jobs.

To display the outputs and goals, we recommend that you use the Job Model format presented in Chapter Eleven. To identify the resources, feedback, rewards, and training that should support the new job responsibilities, we suggest that you use the Human Performance System questions listed in Chapter Six.

This three-step process will enable the participants and others to see the benefits of addressing all Three Levels of Performance. They will work with four of the pivotal Three Levels tools—the Relationship Map, the Process Map, the Job Model, and the Human Performance System questions. Most important, they will resolve a critical issue facing the organization.

We don't, however, want you to think that the Three Levels can be used effectively only in a "bundled" fashion. A second answer to "Where do I start?" is by applying one or two of the Three Levels tools in a targeted application. In addition to the more comprehensive projects described earlier (especially in Chapters Eight and Ten), organizations have successfully applied individual Three Levels tools in ways such as these:

- Relationship and Process Mapping were used to realign an entire telecommunications company to increase the focus on the customer.
- Relationship and Process Mapping were used to strengthen and formalize the historical "handshake" relationship between an electronics manufacturer's U.S. headquarters and a foreign subsidiary, which is projected to quadruple its revenues in three years.
- Relationship Maps were used in an aerospace company's orientation training to quickly show new employees where they fit into the big picture.
- Organization, Process, and Job measures were used in a paper mill to get everyone from the Mill Manager to the machine operators rowing in the same direction.
- Role/Responsibility Matrices and Job Models were used to clarify the responsibilities of Branch Managers in a consumer loan business and to clarify the responsibilities of four levels of management in a 1400-store retail organization.
- The Human Performance System was used by a publishing company to diagnose and remove some of the causes of high turnover among its salespeople.
- Job Models and the Human Performance System were used as the basis for the design of a performance appraisal system in a government agency.

Summary

Our files contain data on over 200 performance improvement projects spanning twenty-five years. They all included applications of Three Levels tools, and they range from the macro (establishing speedy cycle time as a competitive advantage in an international electronics company) to micro (improving the performance of machine operators in a snack-food manufacturing company). We continue to find new ways in which all three categories of users — executives, managers, and analysts — are applying the Three Levels as:

- A *set of tools* for diagnosing and eliminating deficient performance
- An *engine* for continuously improving systems that are performing adequately
- A *road map* for guiding an organization in a new direction
- A *blueprint* for designing a new entity

However, Three Levels performance improvement is more than issue-specific interventions. The tools enable managers and individual contrib-

utors to bring about many of the culture changes that are frequently discussed but rarely pursued systematically. These culture changes include:

- Ensuring that a customer orientation drives all activities
- Establishing accountability by objective performance measurement
- Minimizing departmental conflicts
- Implementing a participative style of management
- Creating a work environment that leads to both better performance and
  a higher quality of work life

We believe that any reader takes no more than a handful of meaningful
ideas or tools from even the best of management books. In our opinion, the
most significant ideas we have presented are:

- Organizations behave as adaptive systems. To effectively, nimbly, and
  proactively adapt to the demands of a rapidly changing environment, all
  system components — inputs, processes, outputs, and feedback — must be
  managed.
- An organization's strategic and operational effectiveness is the product of
  Three Levels of Performance — the Organization Level, the Process Level,
  and the Job/Performer Level. As a result, every improvement effort must
  be seen through the lens of the Three Levels.
- The Three Performance Needs that must be met at each of the Three
  Levels are: Goals, Design, and Management. Failure to manage the nine
  Performance Variables is failure to manage the business holistically.
- Cross-functional processes are particularly critical to the quality, produc-
  tivity, cycle time, and cost of any business.
- Managing people should include addressing the needs of all components
  of the Human Performance System in which they work.
- At each of the Three Levels, there are tools that can help in documenting,
  analyzing, and improving performance.

We are performance improvement practitioners. We are interested in a
theory only if it helps us get results. We have found that the Three Levels
framework provides us with a unifying theory of performance improvement.
More important, it has led us to the tools we have described and illustrated.

In Chapter One, we described what we see as the challenge facing
American companies. A rapidly changing market, higher quality standards,
increasing competition, shortages in critical resources, and mind-boggling
expansion of technology have become the norm in almost all industries.
Traditional solutions do not address this new reality.

The approach we have described does not represent a quick fix. We
have never experienced the use of a tool that brings about comprehensive,

lasting organization change without the investment we have described. The Three Levels viewpoint will enable you to better understand your organization and the variables affecting its performance. With this understanding as a foundation, you can use the Three Levels technique to bring about top-to-bottom performance improvement. We believe that the challenge can be met.

REFERENCES

Deming, W. E. *Quality, Productivity, and Competitive Position.* Cambridge: Center for Advanced Engineering Study, Massachusetts Institute of Technology, 1982.

Gilbert, T. F. *Human Competence: Engineering Worthy Performance.* New York: McGraw-Hill, 1978.

Ishikawa, K. *Guide to Quality Control.* (2nd ed.) Asian Productivity Organization, 1982.

Kane, E. J. "IBM's Quality Focus on the Business Process." *Quality Progress*, Apr. 1986.

Kepner, C. H., and Tregoe, B. *The New Rational Manager.* Princeton, N.J.: Princeton Research Press, 1981.

Manoogian, J. Personal correspondence with G. Rummler, Mar. 8, 1989.

Murphy, J. R. "Process Is Not Strategy: Training Managers to Carry Out a Strategy-Based Quality Plan." Paper presented to the Juran Institute Conference, Chicago, 1988.

Peters, T. J., and Waterman, R. H., Jr. *In Search of Excellence: Lessons from America's Best-Run Companies.* New York: Harper & Row, 1982.

Process Quality Management and Improvement Guidelines. Publication Center, AT&T Bell Labs, Dec. 1987.

BIBLIOGRAPHY

The Foundation

Most of the models ("Organizations as Systems" and the "Human Performance System" in particular) and convictions presented in this book have their origins in the 1960s, when Geary Rummler was working as part of the University of Michigan Business Schools' Bureau of Industrial Relations for George S. Odiorne and with Dale and Karen Brethower, Carl Semmelroth, Al Schrader, Dave Markle, Bill Cave, Mal Warren, Don Smith, Tom Gilbert, and George Geis. The stimulation that contributed to these models came from many sources and in a variety of forms. These authors (and, to a lesser degree, their publications) were major contributors to the concepts and beliefs represented in this book.

Boulding, K. "General System Theory: The Skeleton of Science." *Management Science*, Apr. 1956.

Brethower, D. M. *A Systems Approach to Educational Problems*. Occasional paper, Center for Programmed Learning for Business, University of Michigan, 1966.

Forrester, J. W. "Systems Technology and Industrial Dynamics." *MIT Technology Review*, June 1957.

Geis, G. L. "Retention: A Pseudo Problem." *National Society for Programmed Instruction Journal*, 1966, 5 (2).

Hitch, C. J., and McKean, R. N. *The Economics of Defense in the Nuclear Age*. Boston: Harvard University Press, 1963.

Katz, D., and Kahn, R. L. *The Social Psychology of Organizations*. New York: Wiley, 1966.

Lippitt, R., and others. *The Dynamics of Planned Change*. San Diego, Calif.: Harcourt Brace Jovanovich, 1958.

Mechner, F., and Cook, D. A. "Behavioral Technology and Manpower Development." In *Managing the Instructional Programming Effort*, Bureau of Industrial Relations, University of Michigan, 1967.

Murphy, J. R. "Training Man of the Future." *Training*, 1964, *1*, 1.

Nadler, G. "Is Analysis of the Present System Really Necessary?" *Systems and Procedures*, 1965, *6*, 9.

Odiorne, G. S. "A Systems Approach to Training." *Training Director's Journal*, 1965, *19*, 10, 11–19.

Odiorne, G. S. "The Need for an Economic Approach to Training." *Training Director's Journal*, Mar. 1964.

Rath, G. J. *Behavioral Planning Networks*. ESK–TDR–63–607. Decision Sciences Laboratory, ESD, Hanscom Air Force Base, Aug. 1963.

Silvern, L. C. "A General Systems Model of Public Education K–12." *Educational Technology*, 1963, *4* (12), 1–20.

Silvern, L. C. "Systems Aspect." In *Administrative Factors Guide*. Los Angeles, Calif.: Education and Training Consultants, 1964.

Spicer, E. (ed.). *Human Problems in Technological Change—A Casebook*. Russell Sage Foundation, 1952.

Warren, M. *Training for Results*. Reading, Mass.: Addison-Wesley, 1969.

Further Reading

Our Three Levels framework provides an overview of what we believe to be factors affecting organization performance. In order to control the size of the book and increase its usability, we have not gone into exhaustive detail. We hope your interest will be piqued in some cases and you will want to learn more. Following are our recommendations for further reading:

Systems View

Ackoff, R. L. *Redesigning the Future*. New York: Wiley, 1974.

Ackoff, R. L. *Creating the Corporate Future*. New York: Wiley, 1981.

Checkland, P. B. *Systems Thinking, Systems Practice*. London: Wiley, 1981.

Kauffman, D. L. *Systems One: An Introduction to Systems Thinking*. Minneapolis, Minn.: Future Systems, Inc., 1980.

Organization Level

Aaker, D. A. *Strategic Market Management*. New York: Wiley, 1984.

Hax, A. C., and Majluf, N. S. *Strategic Management: An Integrative Perspective*. Englewood Cliffs, N.J.: Prentice-Hall, 1984.

Ohmae, K. *The Mind of the Strategist*. New York: McGraw-Hill, 1982.

Tregoe, B. B., and Zimmerman, J. W. *Top Management Strategy*. New York: Simon & Schuster, 1980.

Process Level

AT&T Bell Laboratories. "Quality by Design." 1987, *1* (1).

Kane, E. J. "IBM's Quality Focus on the Business Process." *Quality Process*, Apr. 1986.

Time-Based Competition Series. Boston Consulting Group, 1988.

Job/Performer Level

Introduction to Performance Technology, Vol. 1. Washington, D.C.: The National Society for Performance and Instruction, 1986.

Bolt, J. F., and Rummler, G. A. "How to Close the Gap in Human Performance." *Management Review*, Jan. 1982.

Brache, A. P. "Managing Performance Is More Than Managing People." *Business Magazine*, Apr.–June 1989.

Gilbert, T. *Human Competence: Engineering Worthy Performance*. New York: McGraw-Hill, 1978.

Mager, R. F., and Pipe, P. *Analyzing Performance Problems*. Belmont, Calif.: Fearon, 1970.

INDEX